My Love Affair with Bruges

MARGARET OLSEN

BALBOA.
PRESS
A DIVISION OF HAY HOUSE

Balboa Press books may be ordered through booksellers or by contacting:

Balboa Press
A Division of Hay House
1663 Liberty Drive
Bloomington, IN 47403
www.balboapress.com
1 (877) 407-4847

Because of the dynamic nature of the Internet, any web addresses or
links contained in this book may have changed since publication and
may no longer be valid. The views expressed in this work are solely those
of the author and do not necessarily reflect the views of the publisher,
and the publisher hereby disclaims any responsibility for them.

This book is a work of non-fiction. Unless otherwise noted, the author
and the publisher make no explicit guarantees as to the accuracy of
the information contained in this book and in some cases, names of
people and places have been altered to protect their privacy.

Cover art ©2014 by Barbara Olsen
Interior illustrations ©2015 by Barbara Olsen
Author photograph ©2015 by Barbara Olsen

Print information available on the last page.

ISBN: 978-1-5043-4393-0 (sc)
ISBN: 978-1-5043-4395-4 (hc)
ISBN: 978-1-5043-4394-7 (e)

Library of Congress Control Number: 2015918004

Balboa Press rev. date: 02/22/2016

Dedication

To Ed, Harriet, Lislie, and Odette

Contents

Introduction

Returning, returning, always returning to Bruges... Is it so very strange to think that I could have existed here long, long ago? Right here at the Beguinage, a protected place for me back then? And now today, I feel that same peacefulness and protection.

Black clouds moving across the sky, a slight wind blowing the trees, red-tiled roofs, a few birds flying swiftly past my window... Where am I? Why do I feel so content, so secure? I feel like a baby being held in loving arms. Why am I constantly being drawn back?

What is time? Many events could be taking place at the same time in different places, different periods in history. One-dimensional living is so insignificant. How do I enter that world? I was here before. I know I was. I can feel it. Every so often, I catch that whiff of it but it comes so swiftly, I almost miss it. When it happens, I want to hold on to it much longer but it can be so elusive.

How do I go back? Listen for the bells. Go back. Go far back. Draw back the curtain. Let me see.

———

I need to write about my love for Bruges. I need to tell the story of this love affair. When reading Frances Mayes' book, *Under the Tuscan Sun*, a sentence hit me with such a force and stayed with me. It was: "Never casual, the sense of place is something you crave."

What is there in Bruges that I crave? Is it the sense of protection, of close set buildings along the narrow streets, without tall buildings creating wind tunnels? Buildings feel smaller except for the magnificent churches. Winding streets, nothing straight-lined and laid out in precise north, south, east and west directions. Canals, with majestic swans claiming ownership, huge ancient trees, and always the sound of church bells...

What do I crave there? Whatever it is, I get it there! I feel so in-the-moment and peacefulness resides within me. I do not feel like a tourist; I feel like I live there. People even ask me for directions! Why can't I keep that feeling for long periods when I'm back in Canada? Holiday feelings are different, you say. Yes, I realize that but this goes deeper than holiday feelings. No holiday feelings have had this much impact. As Frances Mayes says, in *Under the Tuscan Sun,* "Once in a place, that journey to the far interior of the psyche begins or it doesn't. Something must make it yours, that ineffable "something" – no book can capture."

Do I feel the past within me as I walk the streets of Bruges? Is it the medieval time that I feel? I do not feel that "whatever" when I walk in my city in Canada. In Bruges, I hear it softly calling to me. But I want the calling to be louder as I long to slip back into the medieval world. I must just be grateful for the continual experience of Bruges and thankful that it can always evoke the same feeling within me, a feeling that spreads throughout my body and gives me deep peace and much joy.

Chapter 1

Two Stops Before Norway

E d and I made our first trip to Europe in 1969 and enjoyed it immensely. In 1982, we start to discuss going on another trip to Europe. Ed says, "I'd like to go to Norway this time."

"Oh, you want to explore your roots. Check out your Viking heritage!" He laughs. "Well, I need to do it soon while there are still relatives there to contact."

"Ed, all you need to do is to get the information from your Mom about your relatives in Norway. I'll start reading about Norway and also about other places we might like to go." Ed is not the avid reader that I am but he is happy for me to give him information as we travel.

As it turns out, our geologist daughter Debbie, who lives in Calgary, also expresses an interest in seeing Norway so we arrange for her to meet us in Oslo. Ed says, "With her height and her love of the outdoors, Debbie will fit right in with the Norwegians."

While researching, I become fascinated with Bruges, a medieval city in Belgium. The inner city, surrounded by a canal, has been preserved with buildings and bridges dating back to the thirteenth, fourteenth, and fifteenth centuries. It intrigues me as I had never heard of it and the more I read about it, the more I feel I would love to include it in our trip, and even spend a few days there.

"When would we do that?" asks Ed when I tell him about it.

"Well, we could take the Wardair flight to Amsterdam and explore that city for a few days, then rent a car and drive to Bruges. Afterwards we could return to Amsterdam for our train journey to Copenhagen and on to Norway."

"Okay, I'll go with that. Will we need to make reservations in Bruges?"

"No, I don't believe that many people know about it. I've never heard of it and from what I've read, it is just a quiet medieval town."

In May, we fly eight hours to Amsterdam. I like the vibrancy of the Amsterdam airport as we get our luggage, catch a bus into the city and then take a taxi to our small hotel. Our room is not large but has two lovely windows opening onto a garden with a huge chestnut tree and I can hear birds singing.

Our first time in Amsterdam! Ed asks, "Would you like to go for a short walk?"

"No, I only got a few hours sleep on the plane, so I'm ready for a nap. But you go ahead and I'll have a walk with you later."

I snuggle into bed. I wish that I had Ed's enthusiasm but I'm just too tired to go walking right now. When I awake, Ed is there beside me and as I open my eyes wider and look around, I see a box of fresh strawberries on my bedside table.

"How nice! Where did you get them?" I eat one. "They're delicious. Mmmm."

3

"There is a fruit vendor just a short way from here. He has a stall by the canal, with lovely looking fruit. I thought that you would enjoy the strawberries."

We're close to Vondelpark so we walk there and then onwards through some of the streets. We're amazed at all the cyclists, so totally different from Canada. We walk and walk and, as it starts to rain, we head to the restaurant suggested by our hotel where we get a table by a window.

"Oh, this feels relaxing. I'm hungry, are you?"

"Yes, very. Must be all that fresh air we've had," says Ed.

"Listen, they're playing an American song. I thought we would hear Dutch music and the singing in Dutch, not English. The American influence is everywhere!"

After a delicious meal, we stroll back to our hotel. The rain has stopped and the evening is warm, people are everywhere, on the streets, in the restaurants, and with sounds of music it feels good to be walking among it all.

"What a lot of happy people. What fun. I get the feeling that their evenings are just beginning!" I say.

At our hotel we learn that breakfast is served between eight and ten in the morning. But now, we are off to bed, very ready for a good night's sleep!

We're awakened with knocking on the door. Morning already? I open my eyes and check the time – it's eleven-thirty! I quickly put on a robe and answer the door only to find the maids. I tell them that we have overslept and to come back later. Ed is stretching on the bed and I say,

"We've overslept and missed our breakfast! Just like our first trip to London, when we did the same thing!"

We begin our late start with breakfast at an outdoor café before taking in the Van Gogh museum. In the late afternoon we enjoy a lovely canal ride and in the evening, we choose an Indo-Chinese restaurant hoping to try their specialty, Rijsttafel. The waiter says that it translates to Rice Table. When it arrives it looks very impressive. There is rice surrounded by various little dishes and Ed and I attempt to decide what everything is: peanuts, bananas, water chestnuts, chutney, various cooked vegetables, raisins and peanut sauce to go over it all.

"I'm glad we tried this. It's fun to taste something different and so flavorful," I say.

"Yes, this is delicious," says Ed as he adds more food to his plate.

Seems our internal clocks are on European time now and we manage to make it for breakfast the next morning.

"How about doing the Rijksmuseum today?"

Ed agrees. "Okay, but first I'd like to check out the Heineken Brewery. I read at the hotel that you can take a tour through it."

"That doesn't interest me so much but let's check it out. Maybe I could do something else while you do the tour."

"Remember I worked at the Brewery in Prince Albert? That's why I'm interested now."

"Oh, yes that was like a gap year between your first and second university years!" Later, however, we discover that all the tours are full and that the whole day is already booked.

"I didn't realize how popular a brewery tour would be. You must get to sample beer!" I say.

We walk to a canal where we rest and watch some ducks for a while before going to the Rijksmuseum. It is overwhelming, much more than we expected. A quick lunch stop is essential before continuing our tour of the museum. Finally, worn out we head back to our hotel where I sink into the lovely long bathtub. I come out and say, "I'm ready for a short rest before we go out for dinner. This has been a full day."

"Great idea," says Ed.

We snuggle in but what was meant to be naptime turns into lovemaking. I feel revived and have lovely rosy cheeks! Time to find a restaurant. Again the night is beautiful, a lovely warmth for the middle of May.

"Where do you want to go?" says Ed.

"I would like to go back to the restaurant that we went to on our first night. It was so relaxing and the food was good—and this is our last night in Amsterdam!"

"We could try something different but you're right, it was nice and the food was tasty."

As we walk there I say, "I feel like a beacon with these rosy cheeks."

"Yes" laughs Ed, "everyone will know what you've been doing!"

"Oh, go on with you!" I say and give him a shove.

Next morning, all packed up, we pick up our rental car at the airport. It is a blue Fiat. Ed tries out the lights, the turn signals, and finds the wipers as it is pouring rain. We get out on the highway and begin our drive to Bruges. The rain stops shortly outside of Amsterdam. The countryside is lovely. "I've never seen such enormous cows!" says Ed.

"It is great driving here where the passing lanes are strictly for passing. Canadians, who don't usually move out of these lanes back home, would have a hard time here. They'd certainly get lights flashed at them if they didn't move over."

Chapter 2

First Time in
Bruges - 1982

We continue driving through Rotterdam, Antwerp, Ghent, and finally we cross over a bridge and enter Bruges. As we drive down the narrow cobblestone street, I'm amazed at how busy it is with cars, people, and bicycles. Ed says,

"I thought you said that this was a quiet medieval city that hardly anyone came to!"

"Maybe it is a special day or a celebration or something."

"I don't know where to go here. It's impossible," says Ed as he slowly drives down the crowded street.

"We need to go to the tourist bureau in the market square to see if they can find a hotel room for us."

We arrive but there is simply no parking! Finally we find a spot, leave the car and walk down crowded narrow sidewalks back to the market square. Where have all these people come from? Where is the peacefulness that I read about?

Inside the tourist bureau we join the line-up. We're third. Finally it's our turn and we ask for a hotel room for a couple of nights. The young woman behind the counter looks at us sadly and says,

"This is a Saturday. There are no hotel rooms available in Bruges tonight. Do you have a car?" Ed nods and she says, "Then my suggestion would be to drive to some of the small towns around here and I'm sure you'll find something for tonight."

She gives us a map of the area around Bruges and we walk back to our car. I'm already feeling that nothing will appeal to me. I want to stay in Bruges!

In a small town, we pass a modest brick hotel that doesn't look too bad.

Ed says, "Shall we go and check it out?"

"No, I really don't want to stay there. What a shame we can't get a hotel in Bruges. I would have made advance reservations if I had known it would be this busy!"

"I'll drive on a bit further. You know there is the possibility that we could get a room in a house in Bruges. I know that we said that we didn't want to do that but I'm willing to try it if you are."

"Yes, it is worth a try. Wonder what time the tourist bureau closes. It is getting close to six."

Ed makes a turn and we head back to Bruges. This time we're able to park in the same place and we hurry to the bureau just as they are beginning to close. We go to the counter and get the same woman.

Ed says, "We're back. We've decided that we would like to stay in Bruges. Is there a room available in a private home?"

"No, they are all taken but as you have a car, there is one just outside the Bruges ring road. It's nice. You'll like it." She gives us the name and directions to get there. We thank her and hurry out the door, which is then locked behind us.

"We're fortunate that we decided to go back when we did. A few minutes later and we would have been out of luck!"

As we drive along a tree-lined canal, I watch the other side of the road for the address. When I see it, Ed pulls into a short driveway. The house is rather modern looking with a field behind it. A tall, slim, and enthusiastic looking man answers the door.

"Welcome, I'm Adrian."

We introduce ourselves and he says, "I'll show you to your room." Up the stairs we go to our second floor room, which is immaculate with a double bed, a large wooden wardrobe, a couple of chairs, and a dresser with a mirror.

"The bathroom is just down the hall. I'll let you settle in."

Out the window I can see a field and beyond that a row of tall trees that goes on and on.

"I'm starved! We haven't eaten since our breakfast in Amsterdam!"

"Yes, me too. Let's find out where we can go to eat."

Adrian tells us, "Bruges has wonderful restaurants but this is Saturday and they'll be booked. However, near here is the town of Damme, where there are a number of excellent restaurants. I'll phone and make a reservation for you, if you like."

"That would be great and we can go very soon. We just realized we haven't eaten since breakfast!"

We hear Adrian talking on the phone but of course we don't understand as it is in Flemish. "It is all set. They'll be expecting you in about twenty minutes. It'll only take you about eight minutes to get there."

A woman with dark hair and a round face comes into the room and our host introduces her as his wife. She smiles and shakes hands with us. He explains,

"She doesn't speak as much English as I do so I'll be doing most of the talking!"

Once I have changed into my soft silky sweater and a skirt, we go back down and Adrian tells us the name of the restaurant and how to get there.

"After your meal, you might just want to drive to Bruges and see the lights. At night, it is lit up like a fairyland! Enjoy your meal."

Damme is a small town and we easily find the restaurant.

"We have a reservation," says Ed, but before he can say anything else, the host says, "Oh yes, the Canadians." He leads us to a lovely round table looking out the front window. We sit down and I gaze out the window at a cobblestone square. There is a tall stone building with steps on each side leading up to an immense wooden door. Also on the building is a tower with a large clock, and all of this is silhouetted against a beautiful deep blue sky. I say,

"Isn't that gorgeous! It looks like a painting. I've never seen a sky that shade of deep blue."

We look at the menu and make our decision. I ask the waiter, "What kind of potatoes come with this?"

He replies, "Pommes frits, Madame."

I ask, "Is there any other choice, like baked?"

He looks quite horrified and says, "Pommes frits are a Belgian specialty."

"Oh, in that case, I'll have them."

I look at Ed and say, "Stop smirking, you know that I never eat French fries!"

"I know, but you're in Belgium and they feel that they invented them, so that is the kind of potato you'll be getting here."

We have the leek soup first, which is just delicious, followed by our entrees and our fries, er... "pommes frits."

"How do they compare with fries in Canada?"

"These are excellent. If you don't want all of them, I'll eat them," says Ed.

"I can't believe we're here in Belgium in this lovely restaurant and looking out at this beautiful "picture." I'm sure that we'll always remember this meal."

A couple of hours comfortably fly by. We leave the restaurant after telling them how much we have enjoyed it all.

"Let's drive in and see the lights of Bruges," I suggest.

"Okay and then I'm going to be ready to hit the bed," says Ed and he drives into Bruges, parks, and we walk toward the centrum. It is exquisitely beautiful with all the lights and the reflections in the canals of buildings, trees, and bridges. When we return to our place it is now close to eleven! Adrian says, "Come in and tell me about your evening. Did you like the restaurant?"

"It was great and they gave us a lovely table looking out the front window."

"Yes, Damme is a small town but it has some excellent restaurants. I debated between two restaurants. I like them both."

"They were expecting us and called us 'The Canadians'!" I say.

"Yes, I just told them that I wanted a reservation for two Canadians!"

"Well, we're ready for bed. It has been a busy day," says Ed.

"I'll see you at breakfast. You'll have a great day in Bruges tomorrow. There is so much to see. What time would you like breakfast?"

Ed and I look at each other and Ed says, "Probably between eight-thirty and nine. We want to have a lot of time in Bruges tomorrow." We say good night and climb the stairs to our room.

Next morning we enjoy our breakfast in front of a window looking out on a large willow tree, a farmhouse, a meadow, and cows. It looks so peaceful. Our breakfast is simple with delicious light brown grainy bread, butter and jam, tea for me and coffee for Ed. As we finish, our host looks in the doorway. "I'm just leaving for town. Enjoy your day. See you this evening."

We drive to Bruges and park just outside the ring road and walk into the tourist bureau to get some suggestions on what to see. It is very crowded. We join the shortest line and I say,

"Let's just buy a map and explore on our own."

The woman shows us how the map is numbered and where the important places are shown. With my confident engineer husband holding onto the map, we begin walking narrow streets, streets that twist and turn, streets crowded with tourists who suddenly stop right in front of us and gaze up at a church spire or look around and wonder where they are. We stop and I say,

"Let me glance at the map and see if I can find the place Adrian mentioned. It is a former palace. I can't pronounce the name. It starts with "Gr" and it is close to the Church of Our Lady. Let's go down this way."

More walking and a turn near the church into Groeninge and we come to a museum but it doesn't look like a palace. Ed says, "Let me look, what we want is Gruuthuse."

"So many "G" names!"

Ed and I believe that we're on our way to the palace museum but we don't see it! Ed looks at the map again and, exasperated, says,

"This is so confusing! Nothing runs north and south or east and west. Totally confusing!"

I look up and point, "That looks like a tall church spire so we just need to walk towards it."

When we reach the church we find, tucked in right beside and in back of it, the Gruuthuse Museum, the former fifteenth century palace of the Lords of Gruuthuse. We wander through the many exhibits depicting the daily life of a wealthy family in that era. On the second floor we are amazed to discover that the Gruuthuse family had their own private chapel with windows cut into the wall of the adjoining Church of Our Lady!

"I can't believe it! They could just sit here and attend church services from their very own home. They didn't need to be with the common folk."

"Yes, we'll have to go into that church and look up here from down below," says Ed.

"I'm ready to move on to the church or another museum."

"Okay but I would just like to go up one more floor and see the display of musical instruments."

In what must be the attic we see pianofortes, flutes and clarinets, most made in the seventeenth and eighteenth centuries. Some of the lids of the pianofortes are decorated with paintings. I hear sounds but it is not the instruments and I realize that it must be raining outside and it is raindrops that I hear. It sounds wonderful. I close my eyes and stand listening and it brings tears to my eyes. I look at Ed, wandering among the instruments, seemingly unaware of the rain. I continue to stand and listen to the sound of the rain.

"I'm ready to leave now. Are you?"

"Yes," I say as I slowly follow him towards the steps.

Outside the rain has stopped and we decide to go on a canal boat ride. The boat driver greets the people as they come into the boat and by our responses he becomes aware of our languages. He says,

"I'll speak in German, Italian, Dutch and English. Have I missed anyone?"

This is repeated in all the languages he stated. No one answers so he starts the boat and off we go. I look around at the buildings, trees and bridges and listen when the description is in English. Ed has the map in his hand and he checks it trying to find street signs. I just shake my head at him and relax. He'll never be able to follow these winding canals!

I begin to feel rain—oh no! It gets stronger and umbrellas are passed out. Once they are opened, it is useless to try to see anything. What a disappointment! We pass alongside houses with canal water skirting their foundations. Later I must ask Ed how such houses are built so that they don't get water inside. The boat docks and the driver wishes us all a great day in Bruges.

"Ed, it sounds as if he expects a tip. Do you have change?"

We tip him as we leave and the driver gives me a hand as I get out of the boat. It has now stopped raining so we have lunch outside in the market square with a good view of the very tall belfry.

"I would like to go for a ride in one of those horse drawn carriages."

"Are you sure?" asks Ed.

"Yes, I really want to. You will come with me, won't you?"

"It doesn't appeal much but I might just for you. What I want to do is to climb that belfry, 366 steps, but what a view!"

"It would be better to climb that on a clearer day but with the horse drawn carriage, the weather doesn't matter that much. I see that they give you a blanket to put over your legs. Just think, how romantic!"

"Sounds good, let's go. But tomorrow I want to climb the belfry before we leave for Amsterdam."

The carriages are in the square and we take the next available one. The driver points out various things of interest. I close my eyes and listen to the sound of hooves on the cobblestones. I love it. Ed seems to be enjoying it too and says,

"This is a great way to get around!"

Clip clop, clip clop. I close my eyes and listen. Clip clop, clip clop, clip clop. But all too soon, it ends. We climb down and walk to one of the bridges where we look down at the passing canal boats.

"Lucky people, it's not raining. Now I would like to go and see the thirteenth-century nunnery. What is it called? Look on the map. We should be able to find it easily as we were right near there in the horse and carriage," I say.

"It is called the Beguinage. It will be a nice walk there. I think that I'll be able to find it!"

We walk down a long street filled with bakeries, chocolate shops, baby things: toys, cribs, blankets, mobiles all so nicely displayed, and card shops, tea shops and restaurants. We turn down a very narrow street, then turn right past a café with outdoor tables, and finally over a bridge and through an entranceway into the Beguinage. There is a grassy area surrounded by buildings, white with orange-red roofs. In front of them stand tall poplars all leaning in one direction, and there are a few paths meandering through the grass. Ed looks at me and asks,

"What does this remind you of?"

I look again and say,

"It's the painting by Churchill that we had on our bedroom wall in our house on 74th Avenue."

"This has to be where he painted it. Remember there were a few nuns walking along on the paths."

"How incredible! I don't think that I have it anymore. I had just clipped it out of a magazine. I always liked it."

We walk along the paths. It seems very peaceful. As we come out of a path, groups of tourists are chatting even though there are signs asking for silence.

We return to our room just before seven. Where has the day gone? I feel like having a bath before we go to dinner, so I check with our host. Of course I can have a bath but there is a charge. I'm given a large towel and off I go. Afterwards, I tell Ed about the charge and say,

"In Canada, we wouldn't be charged for a bath but I guess water is more precious here or more expensive to heat, or whatever."

We ask our host about restaurants and again, he suggests one in Damme. Over dinner, we talk about our day and how much we like Bruges. Next morning after breakfast we say our good-byes to our host and drive into Bruges, parking outside the centrum. Our walk into Bruges brings us to the Town Hall, a very old Gothic building, where there are many paintings depicting the city's history. Outside again, Ed says,

"Still not a really clear day but I want to climb the Belfry. How about you?"

"I think not, but I'll buy postcards and write them while you climb."

I write the cards at a counter in the tourist bureau and then go outside to sit on a bench to wait for Ed. I look up at the very high tower. I wonder if any bells will be ringing when he is up there. I'm sure it would be very loud.

Ed arrives back, quite exhilarated. "The view was great!"

"What was the climb like?"

"You can tell that many people have climbed there as the steps are worn down. The climb wasn't bad. I didn't have to rest along the way."

"Great. Are you ready for some lunch? Then I would like to go into the Church of Our Lady. It opens at two so if we eat now that will work out."

"Sounds good. Let's try that little restaurant we passed yesterday on our way to the Beguinage."

We find the restaurant, relax and enjoy our lunch. Afterwards I mail my cards and it is then time for the church to open. It is an enormous building with a beautiful ceiling. Ed is fascinated, looking at the structure, marveling at how it was built. It is an ornate Catholic church, so unlike the Presbyterian Church that I attended while growing up. We walk around inside, moving at our own pace. I walk very slowly, then stop and stand quietly. Suddenly, I feel a warmth flowing through me and tears begin to form. This intense sensation is all too fleeting. I open my eyes, hoping that I might have this feeling again. But, it doesn't happen.

Ed joins me and we go to view the marble statue of the Madonna and Child, so very beautiful. Sculpted by Michelangelo in 1503, it is one of the very few of his sculptures outside of Italy.

We leave the church, walk behind it and over a small bridge, and through a small park.

"It is after three. I think that we should leave for Amsterdam," says Ed.

We walk to our car and as we stand looking back at Bruges, I say,

"Promise me that we'll come back here again."

"Yes," says Ed. "Let's seal it with a kiss."

I feel sad as we leave Bruges. I had such a feeling of peace, as if I belonged there. The car speeds up and we're on our way back to Amsterdam and then to Copenhagen and on to Norway.

Chapter 3

Good News from Bruges - 1984

In December 1982, we receive a Christmas card from the couple that we stayed with in Bruges, and another card in 1983 with some interesting news. Adrian has now retired and bought a small eight-room hotel in Bruges! So, in June 1984, we return to Bruges and stay at his hotel for a week.

Adrian is happy to see us back again and, this time, he is able to recommend a restaurant right in Bruges where we have a delicious meal. Three Americans sitting at a table near us compliment us on our "happiness" and say that it makes them feel good just watching us!

On our walk back to the hotel, I say,

"I love being back in Bruges. I feel very excited."

The following days are filled with lots of sightseeing, revisiting some museums and going for another canal ride, this time in sunshine. I even climb the Belfry with Ed, three hundred and sixty-six steps! But it was worth it as the view is fantastic on this very clear day.

We come back to Bruges again in 1985 and 1986. Often when we would leave the hotel in the morning, Ed would ask,

"Which way do you want to go?"

I would look at him in astonishment and say,

"There is only one way that I want to go and that is to the Beguinage! I feel so drawn there." When I am there the stillness envelops me immediately.

We hurry along the cobblestone streets and eventually go over the small bridge and enter into the courtyard of the Beguinage. Ed goes back outside to the streets of Bruges to be among people, canals, and outdoor cafes while I walk around and around in the tranquility of the Beguinage surrounded by whitewashed houses. These are similar to the houses of the original Beguines of the 1200s. The small church that was built in the 1300s burned down in 1584 and, fully restored in 1602, it stands inside the gates to the Beguinage. The Benedictine sisters now live here, not a lay order like the original Beguines.

I am reluctant to leave and join Ed and the crowds of people. Each time that we have come to Bruges, I always feel that I need to spend more time here! This is the most peaceful place in Bruges for me. The wind rustles the leaves and I hear the church bell calling the sisters to prayer. My walk becomes slower, more meditative. As I continue along I sense that I have been here before.

Just inside the main archway, I see a smaller whitewashed house. I move closer and read the sign saying that it is an original home of a Beguine, and is now a museum. It will be open for another hour. I hurry out through the opening in the archway and walk over the bridge to the small cobblestoned square with cafes and their outdoor tables. I glance around for Ed and spot him sipping a cappuccino. I bend down and say,

"How about a sip?"

Ed holds up the cup and I lick off some of the whipped cream sprinkled with shaved chocolate.

"Yum, delicious!"

"I'll order you one if you want."

"No, I'll just sit with you while you drink it and I'll tell you what I've discovered. There is a museum inside the Beguinage. It has been there for centuries. We can go there and you can look at the construction."

"You want to go today?"

"Yes, I can't wait. It is open for another hour."

"I'll finish this, pay the bill and then we'll go and have a look."

"Let me have one more sip."

Ed hands his cup to me and I take a good long sip before he finishes the rest and then calls the waiter over to bring the bill. Waiters here never, ever bring the bill until you ask for it. We learned that a few years ago after waiting and waiting. I think it is wonderful that people can linger as long as they want over just a cup of coffee. But really, it is never just a cup of coffee or tea as they always bring a biscuit with it or a wrapped square of chocolate.

Back over the bridge and through the archway, a turn to the left and into the small Beguine house we go. The ceilings are so low. There is a table with pamphlets and post cards. We move on into the other two rooms. There are quite a few people in this small space. One of the women, very smartly dressed, is asking questions of the Benedictine sister. The woman is not Dutch or German but American and she has lots of questions. I move through on my own. I certainly didn't expect so many tourists. I go out a door in the back into a walled-in area with a large stone well. Here it is quieter. I sit down on a bench and hear the canal water lapping on the other side of the brick wall. I can see the tops of trees that stand in the close and a tall church steeple. Ed comes out of the house and goes to look at the well and I wonder how many Beguines in centuries past have come out here to fill their buckets with water. It feels so peaceful and protected and yet I can hear the canal water lapping and see treetops and the sky. Ed comes and sits beside me.

"I love it out here. The house was too crowded and I could get no feeling in there but out here, it is different. Do you feel it?"

"Yes, it is very nice out here."

From his answer, I know that he doesn't feel the way that I'm feeling.

"I find that something touches me very deeply here. I can't really explain it but I must sit for a little while by myself. I just want to be silent. Oh no, more people!" Two older women come out and briefly glance around then go back inside.

"I'm going to go back out. You stay as long as you want. I'll wait for you out on the bridge."

"Good, I'll just stay a bit longer. It'll be closing soon."

I watch Ed walk back inside and I sit back on the bench and close my eyes. A very deep peacefulness and a feeling of warmth come over me. Was I ever here before? Why do I feel so completely comfortable here? I want it all to myself. I open my eyes as I hear voices. A man and a woman come out of the house, walk over to the wall and make some comment in Dutch. They glance at me and go back inside. I stay, listening to the water lapping against the brick wall. I look up and see a small window in the wall. It is covered with wooden shutters. It must look out on the canal. I would like to open it but I don't dare. I feel so strongly that I've been here before. Was it in a past life? Was I a Beguine?

A woman and two children come out and I decide to leave and walk through the house and outside. I see a tour group standing in a circle around their guide. I gather that he is talking about the Beguinage but it is not in English so I can't tune in and hear what is being said. Out through the arch I can see Ed standing on the bridge. He is watching a group of swans floating down the canal. They look so majestic, as if they own the canal. When I reach him, we watch the swans as they continue coming towards us and then disappear under the bridge.

Later that evening, in our hotel room, Ed and I look at some of the information about Bruges that we have picked up during our stay.

"Ed, listen to this—the beginning of the Beguinage goes back to 1244 and it was sponsored by Margaret of

Constantinople. Another Margaret in history! I must research some of these famous Margarets, who have the same name as mine. It makes me feel even more of a connection to the Beguinage.

Ed looks up from the brochure that he is holding and says,

"How about going to another museum tomorrow?"

"Fine with me."

"We can go when it opens at ten and then after we can have some fish soup at that place with tables by the canal."

"And then sometime in the afternoon, I just have to go back into the close at the Beguinage."

"Again?"

"I just can't get enough of being there. I want to walk around and around. I only wish that I could be in there after the gates are closed in the evening and there are no tourists walking around. Some of them talk so loudly even though the sign by the entrance requests silence."

"Okay, I'll walk over to the Zand and look at the market," says Ed.

"It's interesting how you go into the heart of the city, into the market with its crowds of people and I go for peace and quiet and preferably no people!"

And yet, Ed does enjoy quiet. He loves being outside and especially out in nature and by a stream where he can fish!

Eventually, I discover that the Beguinage has a few guest rooms. I am elated and go to visit the sister-in-charge, Sister Mechtilde. She is small, probably in her seventies with a warm sparkle in her eyes. I ask about coming to stay there next year. She says that she would be happy to have me if what I want is quiet. She shows me the dining room and the enclosed garden. I am so excited with the thought that I could come on my own!

That night at dinner, we talk about it and decide that next year, I'll come for ten days on my own and stay at the Beguinage and when Ed arrives, we will stay at the hotel for ten days. It all sounds so perfect.

Chapter 4

My First Stay at the Beguinage - June 1987

As the train leaves the Netherlands and enters Belgium, I am filled with warmth and excitement. I watch out the window as the train moves closer and closer to Bruges. The landscape is flat and dotted with many large, lazy-looking cows and a lot of people on bicycles. There are just a few passengers in this train car and they are either reading or talking. I seem to be the only one interested in the passing scenery. Perhaps they all live here and have seen it many times. Do I stick out as a tourist? The train stops at a station and a group of schoolgirls gets on. They take up a number of seats and chatter loudly. I wish that I could understand what they are saying. They probably understand and speak English. I think it would be wonderful if I knew other languages. I know a little French but that doesn't help me now, nor does the Latin that I took in high school. We pass Essen. It will not be long now until Bruges. I watch out the window hoping to spot the church steeple, the highest point for miles and miles.

Finally, once again, I'm in Bruges. I manage to hoist my suitcase down from the upper rack and hold on to it as well as a carry-on bag and my purse as I step down from the high train step and then onto the platform. It feels good to be in the open air but I still have to go down inside the station and then to the outside. I juggle my luggage getting a good grip on it and walk over to the stairs, a long flight of concrete steps going down into the station. Now I must take great care while descending the steps as I'm beginning to feel the effects of the nine-hour flight and my four-hour train journey, including changing trains. It is late afternoon here but probably after midnight in my time! Even though it was an overnight flight, I didn't sleep on the plane at all. I missed the comfort of having Ed beside me. But I wanted to have some time here on my own, to absorb it all and have the luxury of going where I want to and staying in my special places without having to be concerned about someone else and their plans. I reach the bottom of the steps and walk past the signboards listing trains, departures and arrivals.

There are many people everywhere carrying or pulling luggage and rushing, rushing. The station does not have the peacefulness and tranquility of Bruges. I move on and reach a glass door, which I manage to push open. No doors automatically open for you here. I'm now in the front area of the station, ticket sellers on one side, a candy seller on the other. I glance at the candies: orange, yellow, green, and red ones, caramels, and wrapped chocolates. I love the yellow candies, delicious lemon flavor. But I will have to wait to buy them as I don't want to put down my luggage and search in my purse for my Belgian money. I'll walk down here in a couple of days and get some.

I hurry through the heavy front door, held open by a young man, then walk over to the group of taxis along the curb. At the first one in line, the driver comes out of the car and puts my luggage into the trunk, then opens the back door for me. I get in, feeling grateful that the plane flight and the train ride are over and I've made it this far on my own. I take a deep breath and relax. The driver turns around and looks at me and I say in English,

"To the Beguinage, please."

He nods and, leaving the station area, he drives over a bridge and into the medieval city of Bruges. I know where I am and watch with pleasure as he drives down the cobblestone streets and past shops and narrow sidewalks crowded with people. He stops outside the gate of the Beguinage, turns and says,

"Here's the Beguinage."

"Aren't you driving me inside to the front door?"

"No, taxis aren't allowed in there. You will have to walk in."

I pay him the 135 francs and he takes my luggage out of the trunk. Through the gate, I attempt to pull my suitcase on the cobblestones but it is too difficult. I pick it up thinking that surely I can carry it this last distance. The sky is getting darker and rain is starting to fall. Even with the rain and having to carry my luggage, I feel happy to be here. I take the path across the lawn and through the trees and cross over the cobblestone road to the white building with the huge oak door. I stand on the step and ring the bell.

The door is opened by one of the sisters. She asks me to wait. When Sister Mechtilde arrives, she greets me with a hug and I follow her up the stairs to my room on the second floor.

"I gave you one of the few rooms with hot and cold water because you came all the way from Canada!"

She opens the door, gives me the key, tells me the time of the next meal, and then leaves me to explore my new "home." It is probably the smallest room that I have ever stayed in. There is a narrow bed, a sink, a small closet, a writing table and two chairs, both wooden and straight backed. A window looks out on the back lawn and garden, which is surrounded by high brick walls. The sunlight flooding into the room wraps it in a welcoming glow.

It feels good to be in the room and to know that I won't be disturbed. I put my books, paper and pens on the table. I can sit here and turn slightly to look out the window. The desire is there to organize and plan my time but this is not what I want to do. I want to go deep within and listen to my intuition.

I have no commitments except to be present for the three daily meals. The guests are given white napkins that are placed inside a wooden napkin ring with their room number on it.

Sister Mechtilde places the napkins on the table and the guests sit where she has placed them. After a few meals, I begin to appreciate what a great job she does of placing people next to each other who speak the same language and who, perhaps, have a common interest. The first lady I sit beside is from Canterbury and on my other side is a Japanese lady who speaks a little English.

The meals are tasty and are served by two of the sisters. Always there is soup with both lunch and dinner, though it is really dinner at noon and a light supper at night. To drink with the meals, there is bottled water and bottles of light beer! I'm so surprised to find beer being served here but this is Belgium. Beer is very popular and many different kinds are made in Belgium, some of the best made by Trappist monks.

I eat, I sleep, I walk, and I meditate. I spend a lot of time by myself for the first six days. I realize that the feeling I have is one of absolute security, like a baby being lovingly held. I find that I'm living totally in the moment and discover that when I truly live in the moment, I seem to have more time! Home seems far away. I seem to be so centered right here in Bruges, in the Beguinage.

At supper one night, a woman beside me is speaking Dutch and my seatmate suggests that she can translate for me. She faithfully delivers the gist of each statement as the conversation evolves. After some time, I answer the Dutch woman before the translation is given. My translator stares and says, "I thought you didn't understand Dutch!" I simply reply, "I don't." I had no idea how I knew what the woman was saying but it was all so clear to me at that moment. However, my translator terminated her services and this abrupt disconnection left me to my own thoughts. How was it that I understood? Did I know Dutch long, long ago?

June seems to be a rainy month here. Previous to this stay, sunny weather was always very important to me. Yet, here in Bruges, the weather somehow doesn't matter anymore. I put on my beige raincoat, take my blue umbrella and go walking in the rain. I accept that I can't stop and sit on the wet benches.

In my small room on the second floor, I gaze out my window at the rain pouring down on the grass, the garden, and the brick wall and I love it. And then, when the rain finally stops and I go outside, there is the lovely fresh smell, and moisture in the air. Why am I not crying out for sun? Why am I so acceptant of the weather here?

I sit at my table and start to read some of Joseph Campbell's book on mythology. Fascinating! I underline *"Myths are clues to the spiritual potentialities of human life – what we are capable of knowing and experiencing within."* The rain continues and I read on absorbed in mythology. I glance at my small yellow alarm clock—a quarter to four, almost time for tea. I get up, stretch and run a brush through my hair. Tea is just the thing for such a rainy day!

I decide to ask Sister Mechtilde if she knows of anyone who could speak with me in English about the history of the Beguinage. She answers that she knows someone and will look into it for me. A couple of days go by and I feel sure that she may have forgotten, as she is so busy. In the early afternoon as I sit in the back garden, the sun is out and it feels lovely and warm. But "something" tells me to go back inside. I do and meet Sister Mechtilde, who says,

"I was just looking for you. I know a Dutch lady who speaks English. She lives in one of the small houses here in the Beguinage. I will take you there now."

Once she has introduced me to the Dutch lady, Lislie, Sister Mechtilde leaves. Lislie is very tall, and holds herself with a youthful, erect posture. Her white hair, drawn back into a bun, frames her blue eyes and high cheekbones. A wrinkled face shows the depth of character and warmth of this very handsome woman. We seem to click immediately.

Lislie makes tea and we sit down to it and delicious fruit tarts. She looks at me and says,

"You are a protected soul."

"What?"

"You know that, don't you?"

"Yes. I guess I am."

I tell her about my experience in Hawaii, of being swept far out in the waves and how I survived. Also about the time that I was driving my car and didn't see the red light and entered a busy intersection with cars coming both ways but somehow I came through it. It was as if my car was picked up and lifted through the intersection.

We talk nonstop on a deep level, about beliefs, about soul mates and, oh yes, even some of the history of the Beguinage! I also learn that she is an artist, a musician, and that this very intelligent and vibrant woman is seventy-nine years old. I can't believe it, but I know that I have to get back to Bruges again soon! Seventy-nine seemed "old" to me at that time, as I was only fifty-three. We continue to talk and drink our tea. She says,

"My goodness, it is almost five-thirty. Would you like a glass of sherry?"

"I would love that."

We have our sherry and continue to talk. I glance at my watch and say,

"Oh, it is time for me to leave. It'll soon be time for the evening meal at the Beguinage."

Before I leave we hug and I feel warm and alive. As I walk back to the Beguinage, I find it hard to believe that I arrived at Lislie's at three and it is now six-fifteen!

Two more nights in my little room. I have grown to love it. No one comes into it; nothing is touched or disturbed. After the evening meal, I walk in the courtyard. It is so peaceful, with no tourists, and tonight there is almost a full moon.

The next morning I again meet with Lislie. We exchange addresses as we plan to write to each other. She has cards made up with her illustrations of scenes of Bruges. I buy a set from her.

My last evening, I again walk on the paths in the courtyard. I walk in the moonlight. I feel so peaceful. My last night, alone. Can I take this beautiful, peaceful feeling away with me?

On my last morning at the Beguinage I walk beside the lake, by the canal, through the trees, thinking that perhaps, "this is the end." But no, it seems to me that this has been, and is, a beginning. I'm on my way, my path. What an exhilarating feeling!

I return to my room for a quiet mediation. Behind my closed eyes, I see an image of a balloon slowly soaring upward. Something is opening up for me and becoming clearer.

My desk is cleared, clothes and books are packed and the room now seems an impersonal one, no longer mine. It is time to go. I close the door to my little room, pick up my suitcase with one hand and put my carry-on and purse over the other shoulder. I walk down the narrow carpeted hallway with the creaky floorboards and go down one flight of stairs to the large front door. Sister Mechtilde is there and she kisses me on both cheeks, holds my hands and says,

"I have enjoyed your gentle nature and I hope that you got the quiet space that you wanted."

"I've liked being here and hope to return next year, and thank you for introducing me to Lislie. May I leave my luggage here? Ed and I will return shortly to get it."

"That will be fine. Just put it over here by this doorway."

Chapter 5

Arrivals - June 1987

E d and I have arranged to meet at one of our favorite spots at two o'clock. He should have arrived by now and checked into the hotel. We have been apart for eleven days! I hurry down the path, out the Beguinage gate and along the walk by the lake, over a bridge and turn left down a slanting cobblestone walk and then turn left again and up two steps to a cobblestoned area with three benches, one on each side and one in the middle looking out on the Minnewater, the Lake of Love. There are trees near the benches, sunlight shimmering on the lake and the sky is a brilliant blue, and this is where we are to meet. I don't see Ed. Thoughts run through my head—was his plane late or did he miss the early train? I walk a few steps, look down the path, and then I see him. He has on a bright yellow V-necked sweater with a white collared shirt under it and grey pants. We hurry toward each other and hug and kiss and hug again. Oh, I have missed him!

Later at a café, sitting at an outdoor table by the lake, we order two cappuccinos. Ed loves them but I am not so fond of them. However, the ones here are delicious and come accompanied by a small biscuit.

"How was your time at the Beguinage? Did you like being there?"

"It was marvelous, so peaceful and quiet. I was one of the lucky guests who had hot and cold water in my bedroom. There are only four rooms that have the hot water. Ed, guess what we had to drink at lunch and dinner?"

"Tea?"

"No. Beer!" He looks astonished. He likes beer. I never drink it.

"Did you try some?"

"Yes, I shared a bottle with one of the guests a couple of times. My stomach needed a change from the bottled bubbly water. Isn't it amazing that I go to Belgium, stay with the Benedictine sisters and learn to drink beer? How do I look after my stay there?"

"Peaceful."

Ed pays the bill and we walk back to the Beguinage to get my luggage. I no longer have my front door key so I ring the bell. It is answered by one of the local women who come to clean. There is no sign of Sister Mechtilde so we simply collect my luggage, leave, and walk to the hotel. As we walk under an overhanging tree branch, we stop and have a quick kiss and Ed says,

"I like your hair style."

I laugh and say, "It is quite full and curly from all the rain!"

When we reach our hotel we go upstairs to our room where the first thing I notice is a beautiful bouquet of large yellow lilies. I look inquiringly at Ed and he nods,

"Yes, I bought them for you."

We hug and kiss. We hear the rain beginning to fall and agree to stay in for the afternoon. It only takes a look and soon we are into bed making love, and how the time flies! Much later it is time for dinner and we decide to go to Rambo's restaurant. He warmly greets us, happy to see us back in Bruges again. Ed and I talk and talk.

"We have a lot to catch up on," I say, "plus we just have three more days on our own before Barbara and Stephen arrive."

Our daughter Barbara and her husband Stephen are holidaying in England. They have told us, "On our way to Greece, we'll come to Bruges for a few days as we just have to see what "this Bruges" is like—this place that you are so drawn to!"

The next afternoon, I take Ed to meet Lislie. We arrive around four and I find that Ed too enjoys Lislie. Our conversation seems endless and it is close to seven-thirty when we leave, and eight-thirty by the time Ed and I are at dinner. This is quite the change from my routine living at the Beguinage.

It is an on-and-off rainy day when Barbara and Stephen arrive at the train station. I was hoping for sunshine but it is great to see them. Happily, the rain holds off while we all walk back to the hotel.

Several days of fun begin: lots of walking, a canal boat ride, visiting churches, and browsing through museums. Stephen wants to see the view from the Belfry and so he and Ed climb the stairs while Barbara and I look through an art gallery. Barbara has always had a love of art. Stephen is curious about many things in Bruges. He says,

"I've been reading about some of the food specialities in Belgium and one of them is waffles. I would love to try some."

We have breakfast at the hotel and around noon we decide to go and try some waffles. Unfortunately we're told that they don't serve waffles until two o'clock! In Belgium, waffles are not a breakfast or a lunch food but more of a dessert or something to have with afternoon tea. We do eventually enjoy some crisp Belgian waffles and discover that they are not served with syrup but with icing sugar or whipped cream or fruits. Delicious!

One day when the rain seems to have stopped, we decide to have a picnic on the grassy area along the canal. We buy chicken, buns, wine, beer and strawberries for this feast! But just as we are leaving the hotel it begins to pour rain and so we end up having a fun picnic in our hotel room!

Sadly the day comes when Barbara and Stephen must leave and we go to the train station with them. While we exchange our good-bye hugs, they tell me how much they have both enjoyed Bruges and can see why I love it so much. We stand on the train platform and wave good-bye as the train begins to move. It is sad to see them leave but we cheer up soon as the evening turns out to be sunny and we are able to enjoy a lovely meal outdoors. Sitting by the canal we have a delicious Belgian speciality, Waterzooi. Now this stew is typically made with chicken but when it originated in Ghent it was made with fish.

Tomorrow we leave for Amsterdam where we will stay overnight, then leave the next day to fly home to Edmonton. It's hard to believe that, once again, my time in Bruges is coming to an end... but I will be back next year!

Chapter 6

My Second Stay at the Beguinage - September 1988

I arrive at the Beguinage and Sister Mechtilde greets me with a kiss on each cheek. She is looking great even though she does so much. Last year when I would make a late trek down the squeaky hallway to the bathroom, I would pass her office. I could hear her typing away answering inquiries regarding accommodation and writing up the bills for guests who are leaving. Always she is up early for prayer and then is at our breakfast where, as usual, she has placed our napkin rings with our room numbers, at the places where she wants us to sit.

My room this time is just beside the one I occupied last year and once again I have hot and cold running water! I'm so happy that I again have a room looking out on the back garden with its lawn, flowers, and trees. On my desk, I see a large bouquet of pink gladiolas and a note from Lislie welcoming me to beauty and peacefulness. How thoughtful of her! On the front of the card is a sketch that Lislie has made of the Beguinage area. We have written many letters to each other during the past year and I look forward to seeing her tomorrow.

Early the next afternoon, I leave the Beguinage for Lislie's place. We hug and chatter and then I settle down on her comfortable couch and ask her to play piano for me. She sits on the piano stool. What wonderfully straight posture for an eighty-year-old! I lean back and close my eyes as she begins to play, one piece and then another. It is so beautiful. I begin to feel tears forming. Her piano playing has such feeling to it, nothing sounds set and mechanical, as it is the emotional feeling of the piece that takes over. She ends the piece and for a moment, I don't speak. And then,

"Lislie, that last piece was beautiful. It brought tears. What was it?"

"That was Chopin. He composed some beautiful music."

"Don't stop playing. I'd love to hear more."

"Listen to this and I'll tell you about it after," and she proceeds to play and I listen. It is quieter and different from the Chopin. She finishes and asks,

"What did you think of that?"

"I found it rather soothing."

"That was Brahms, an intermezzo, "Sleep Quietly My Child." I played it at my husband's funeral. Brahms was a favorite of his."

"Was that difficult for you to play at his funeral?"

"Not really. I'm so used to playing. I played a lot of Brahms for him while he was ill. He had bone cancer. What a slow death that is. I cared for him at home. I was exhausted. But enough playing for now, I'm going to boil some water and make us another pot of tea."

"I love this passionfruit tea. Is it a Dutch tea?"

"No. It's a Pickwick tea, made in England. I can't buy it here in Bruges but I can get it when I go to The Hague. It's a real tea, not an herbal."

"I didn't think that it was herbal. I prefer real tea over herbal."

"Any new guests at the Beguinage?"

"Yes, a group of German ladies arrived last night. They were so noisy in the hallways. I think that the sound is even louder when I don't know the language!"

"Oh, those Germans are always noisy. One always knows when they are around. Sister Mechtilde must be busy."

"Yes, very. At breakfast, she put all the German ladies together. They chattered so loudly that I could hardly hear the English lady beside me. I'm amazed at Sister Mechtilde's energy. You did tell me that she was in her seventies, didn't you?"

"That's right. A few months ago, she celebrated her fiftieth anniversary of being a nun! Imagine going four times a day to church for fifty years! When I was in hospital last December, she rode on her bicycle to visit me. It was a dark, dreary December day and I thanked her for coming and expressed my concern about her being out on this kind of day, and also because it was a fair distance for her to come. She assured me that she was happy to do the trip and she looked it, too. How rarely she gets to go out."

"She bikes? How incredible! Women in Canada just don't do that at her age."

"I still ride my bicycle."

We continue to drink tea and talk until I glance at my watch.

"I must go, almost time for supper. I can't believe how fast the time flies when I'm here visiting you! I feel as if I've always known you."

"Well, we are soulmates, you know. Just once in a while that happens. It doesn't seem to matter how long you're away from each other because once you're back together, it is still there and you just move back into that comfortable space."

I carry my cup and some plates to the kitchen and Lislie says,

"Leave that."

"No, I'll just carry some out, less for you to do."

In the hallway we hug each other. I gaze over her shoulder at the very large ornate gilt-edged mirror. Beneath it is a vase of flowers.

"Your flowers are lovely. Thanks again for the bouquet that was in my room when I arrived."

"The flowers along my side wall are doing well. I have some roses just beginning to bloom. Come outside and I'll cut one for your room."

She gets a little knife and we go outside to her rose bush. There is one rose fading away and two are just beginning to unfold.

"Choose one," says Lislie. I do and she cuts it and gives it to me.

"Watch out for thorns. I'll be in after three tomorrow if you want to come over for a visit."

"That would be great. Will you play some more for me?"

"We'll see."

"I must go. See you tomorrow."

As I walk on the cobblestones and across the path through the lawn, I put the pretty deep pink rose up to my nose and breathe in its subtle scent. Back in my room, I move the bouquet of gladiolas to the wide windowsill and put the rose on my desk, a little more beauty for my tiny, sparse room.

The next afternoon, I settle comfortably into Lislie's cream-colored couch, such luxury after my hard straight-backed chair in my room at the Beguinage. Our conversation is about music and instruments. Lislie has a piano in her living room and a small organ in her bedroom. She plays both beautifully. She asks,

"Do you play piano?"

"I took some lessons when I was young but my teacher didn't insist that I keep the proper timing. I can read music but my timing is not right."

"How about playing something for me? I have some music here that you can try."

I never play for anyone but I get up and go to the piano. She finds some easy music for me and I sit down and play. After I stop, Lislie says,

"You have a very nice touch."

I'm thrilled to hear this. I expected her to say, "Yes, I see what you mean, you have no sense of timing."

"But my timing?"

"If I had you for a pupil, I could correct your timing. But what I'm saying is that you have a nice touch and believe me I know what I'm saying. Some people do not have that."

I feel happy. She knows so much about piano playing and has taught people to play and she wouldn't say that I had a nice touch if she didn't believe it!

"Come and play a duet with me. You just have to deal with one hand."

I go to the piano, feeling very nervous but she is encouraging and I begin to relax.

"If you want, I can help you with your playing. We could do some each day. You could surprise Ed when he comes. You and I will play a duet for him."

The next day in the late afternoon, I'm back at Lislie's. We sit down at the piano and play a duet. As we play, she counts out loud and I begin to be conscious of the timing. We play for quite a while. I get tense at times but then start to relax as the notes become more familiar to me and I begin to get a sense of the timing. Lislie says,

"I'll go and make some tea. You keep on playing."

I timidly continue playing and occasionally, she calls out,

"Wrong note," or, "Stay on that note. Remember to count."

She comes back with the tea and freshly squeezed orange juice.

"Have some juice. I'm sure that you don't get enough fresh fruit at the Beguinage."

We sit and drink tea out of her blue-edged white porcelain cups and eat some cookies.

"How is it that your music teacher didn't stress the right timing?"

"Well, my first teacher just lived a few houses from us. She lived with her sister and they both were what we called "old maids." She just taught me notes and let me play. When I practiced at home, my mother never said anything. I don't think she liked to listen to me practicing. She never told me to practice, not like at my friend Elaine's house. Her mother was always telling her to practice and noticed what she was playing and sometimes complimented her. Elaine couldn't come out to play unless her practicing was finished for that day."

"Was this woman your only teacher?"

"She was for the first couple of years and then we moved and Mom started me with Mrs. Novak, a lovely white-haired lady who also played the organ at one of the churches. I really liked her and she seemed to take an interest in me and tried to help me with my timing. But by then, the bad habits I'd learned were hard to change. I took lessons from her for a short time and then my parents decided to stop my lessons and I don't think that I minded too much. Now, of course, I wished I had stayed with Mrs. Novak. She was a caring person."

We finish our tea and I get ready to leave.

"Come back tomorrow and we'll play again. You really should get back into it. If you lived here, I could have you playing very well in a few months."

"I'm intrigued. I would love to be able to play. It is interesting that Ed has started taking lessons. He had never played before and couldn't even read music. For years, he had talked about taking up the piano but it wasn't until I started saying that I thought that I would take piano lessons again that he went and found a teacher and started taking lessons. So now if I start taking music, we'll have to share playing time!"

"Well, come tomorrow and we'll get on with it."

We hug and I go down the path to the huge wooden door. I insert my key into the lock, turning just the right amount and the door opens. My room faces west and the last of the sun is flooding in and giving warmth to my room. I have time to read before I go down for dinner. I feel excited thinking back to the piano playing and look forward to tomorrow.

The next morning I am happy to go for a walk with just a cardigan and not a raincoat. I like this September weather better than June of last year. I walk and walk. It feels so good to be back here and to know that I have another eight days on my own. I keep waiting to have my beautiful Bruges feeling that I experienced here last time. But I can't force it. I feel like an empty vessel waiting to be filled. I keep thinking about how I felt last time but I need to realize that this is a different time. I too, am different than I was last year. I turn and head back. It is almost time for lunch except I know that it will not be a mere lunch but a dinner complete with soup, main course and dessert. I'm hungry and ready for it!

Back in my little room, I know I can write, read or just sit and look out the window at the large flower garden, the grass, the trees and all this surrounded by the high brick wall. Above it, I see the blue sky and church spires and they beckon me out for a walk before I go to see Lislie.

I walk beside the canals. There is always water and trees, so peaceful and comforting. Why do I like it here so much? Why am I constantly drawn here? Why do I cry when I leave? I go off the main path to a tiny cobblestoned area and up two steps to three benches. I sit on the one closest to the water. There are ducks and mud hens floating on the lake, but there are no people on the lake as no swimming or boating are allowed here. Across the lake are tall, stately trees lining the water and there are also a couple of benches. I've sat on those benches too, but I prefer this bench where it is more secluded. Often, I can sit for quite awhile without being disturbed by people, though they really do not invade my space as they treasure their space too.

As I sit, my mind goes back to Christmas and the unwrapping of a very large gift from my oldest daughter, Debbie. I pull away the last bit of paper to see that it is a poster-style photograph. It was taken from a bridge over a canal and by the color of the leaves, it looks like a fall scene and, I know where it is!

"Debbie, how special! It is Bruges. Wherever did you find this?" Debbie smiles.

"I knew you would like it. I bought it in September in a small shop in Denver when I was there for a Geology conference."

"Like it? I love it and I know just where this has been taken, the exact bridge. I love standing on this bridge and looking at this scene," I say in the excited voice that I get whenever I talk about Bruges. Debbie looks pleased. It is uncanny the way that she can choose gifts that are so perfect and so unexpected.

A couple of days go by. The group of German women has left and now there are three English ladies. I've had some good conversations at meals with two of them, Freda and Betty. The other is Mrs. Rosen, who I met last year and she was so happy to see me again. She was born in Turkey, married an

Englishman, but is now a widow living in London. She had given me a small box of chocolates from Sukerbuyc, telling me that they had the best chocolates in Bruges and that the shop's name means *Sugarbelly* in English.

It is all so pleasant but I know that I need, and want, to take more time for myself. Tune into my center, my being. It is happening but seems slower than last year. But it is a different year and I know that I will find my space.

I told Lislie that I would visit her tonight so that is what I'll do. She is happy to see me and we hug. She has made jam today and looks a little tired but we talk and talk and before I know it, it is time for me to leave. Lislie says,

"I'm going to give you some bread and cheese and bottled water and then you can sleep in and miss breakfast."

I have mixed feelings about this as I did enjoy breakfast this morning and besides Mrs. Rosen is leaving tomorrow morning so breakfast would be my last time to see her. But I thank Lislie and now I'll have something to snack on in my room if I want to!

It's close to ten, time to leave. It is a lovely evening with a full moon and as I slowly walk along I feel drawn to the path across the lawn. I just don't feel like going inside right now. I'll just walk a little more around the close and then go in.

When I go to the big oak door I discover that it is already double-locked. Oh no! It is after ten. What do I do? I look up at the windows above me and see that Betty's is partly open. I call her name again and again under her window and eventually she looks out and I ask her to please open the front door! She does and invites me to her room where she and Freda have been visiting. Betty makes me a cup of tea and I sit and chat with them. What enjoyable women they are. I go back to my room and it is eleven-thirty! Although I go to bed, I don't get to sleep for hours. After all, it was quite a stimulating evening, with good conversation, a walk in the moonlight, getting locked out, and finally being rescued.

Next day at ten, as pre-arranged, Lislie and I take a taxi to the fifteenth-century Die Swaene Hotel to attend a concert featuring a French horn quartet. The performance is delightful, staged in very elegant surroundings and with Belgian champagne served afterwards!

Later our lunch at an outside table includes clam bisque, crusty bread and a glass of red wine, all delicious. On the way back we stop at the Memling Museum. It is a special treat to have the art explained by Lislie as she is an expert, having given lectures on art.

Back in my room that same evening, I decide to move my table right in front of my window. I like that much better. The nicest time seems to be late afternoon and early evening when the sun shines into my room. What shifts I'm having—meditating and calming here and then I go to Lislie's and it's all so stimulating. What a yo-yo effect it has but perhaps I can handle it. I want both at this time.

Time is flying by. Lislie has given me copies of some of the piano pieces so that I can practice them at home. I'm getting down to my last few days before Ed arrives. Last night, I walked around in the close for over a half hour and felt like walking longer but I didn't want to be locked out, especially now that Betty and Freda have left. I am feeling good. I realize that what I had here last year was a mystical experience. I was on such a high plane and yet my emotions seemed so calm, like a still lake. I hope to have that again sometime.

Now it is the day before Ed arrives and it is raining! I hope it stops before his arrival tomorrow, but he does seem to bring sunshine! I'm off to have afternoon tea and visit with Lislie. We hug and settle in to tea, talk and laughter. She asks,

"Could you and Ed come here on Monday for tea? And also on Wednesday, I've set up a lunch and some time for us in the countryside outside of Bruges. My friend Harriet, who has a car, will drive us!"

"It sounds great. I'm sure Ed will like it, too."

My last night, and it's too rainy to walk in the close. I'm sorry that this time I didn't get to hear the sisters sing, as I've enjoyed hearing their Gregorian chant, but the time just wasn't right. Next time I'll go to the five-thirty Choral Vespers. It is the service that I like best. Nice to hear that I've said, "Next time!" Now I'll go to bed early and have a long read. It hasn't really registered that I'm leaving tomorrow. Poor Ed, having to get over jet lag!

Next morning, I go for a lovely walk and carry my umbrella but I don't need it. I have great hopes for sun when

Ed arrives. I have a lovely feeling while walking. I feel very calm yet I sense a rapture for living. I feel ready to be back in my life again, not like last year when I was not ready. I was in a beautiful, calm, peaceful state, but knew that could not be maintained in the outer world.

Ed arrives and it is a sunny day! A couple of days later, we are at Lislie's for tea, and she says,

"Margaret has a little surprise for you."

Lislie and I go to the piano and play our duet. We finish and I turn and look at Ed. He looks amazed and says,

"Very nice!"

"Lislie has been helping me with my piano playing!"

"Ed, I hear that you're taking piano lessons. Will you play something?"

Ed sits down at the piano and plays a simple version of a light classical piece that he has memorized.

"Good for you. Do you want to play some of my music? I have pieces that you could play." But Ed declines the offer.

Chapter 7

Meeting Harriet - 1988

On Wednesday, as has been arranged, Ed and I go to Lislie's. She says,

"Harriet and her goat will be here soon. We're going to drive out of Bruges into the countryside to an inn and you must see the garden. It is planted in such a beautiful way, a magnificent arrangement of color. It is obviously done with an artist's eye!"

Harriet arrives in her car, the so-called "goat." Harriet, at about sixty-years-of-age, has a very fresh, youthful complexion and short blond hair. I like her immediately. She calls Lislie, Lizzie.

We drive out of Bruges, past farms, and cows and cows, along rows of trees, and through small towns with very prominent churches. We arrive at the Inn and discover that it is closed due to a private function. I am disappointed and think how disappointed Lislie must feel after telling us about it and creating expectations in us. But it doesn't faze her, she just says,

"Oh, that is too bad. I did so want to eat there and see the interior but there is another place down the street and we'll go there instead."

So we leave, our excitement still with us. We enter the restaurant and are shown to a table by the window. Harriet and Lislie do the ordering. We eat, laugh, and talk and talk. At one point, we are deep into a conversation about homosexuality. It suddenly seems quite quiet. A young couple, who obviously understand English, are sitting near us and listening intently!

After lunch, we walk to the colorful flower garden at the Inn. It is a beautiful display of colour: pinks, mauves, blues, and reds all blending and yet also holding their own. Once back into the "goat," Harriet drives us to Osstcamp, the town where she grew up, and shows us a very old, beautiful church with a high tower.

Next, Harriet drives us to the site of a very old abbey. It is no longer there, but the ancient oak-beamed barn, where travelers bedded down in medieval times, still stands. It is one of the few rural buildings in all of Europe that is more than seven hundred years old! We get out and walk around and into the barn. The enormous ceiling looks like the inside of an overturned boat. Ed is fascinated with the structure and the materials.

Harriet asks, "Would you like to go back to my place in Bruges for tea?"

We all agree and I wonder where it is in Bruges that Harriet lives. As we get close to Bruges, she drives near the center of the city and down a narrow cobblestone street. Harriet lets us out in front of a deep blue door and drives the goat down to the end of the street to park it. That done, she walks back, opens the door and we enter the hallway. There is a table along the left-hand wall with a lovely bouquet of flowers in front of a large mirror. We continue down the hall past doors on the right and a staircase on the left. I walk on into the kitchen, past the counters, a stove, and right to the end where there is a table with chairs in front of a window looking out on the canal. I'm elated! I'm in a house by the canal! Not only that but I have the strongest feeling that I've been in this house before, especially sitting in this kitchen by the window!

"I knew you would like it here in Harriet's kitchen," says Lislie.

Harriet makes the tea and we all sit in the kitchen by the window, drinking tea and eating chocolate covered cookies. I see canal boats going past filled with tourists and the driver telling them about the wonders of Bruges. Some of the tourists look up and see me in the window and they must think that I'm a real Belgian lady in my home! I love it. I feel so happy here.

Later, Harriet asks me if I would like to see some more of the house. I, of course, say yes!

We climb up the stairs to the second floor. There is a bathroom and a guest bedroom near the front. Harriet's bedroom is in the back overlooking the canal and beside her room is a small room with bookshelves, a single bed and a desk near the window with a view of the canal. Harriet pushes open the shutters and when I lean out and look to the left and further down, I see a bridge that I often stand on looking down the canal at the houses alongside.

"Harriet, I can't believe it! I really like that bridge and last Christmas, my daughter Debbie gave me a poster of Bruges and it showed this very bridge and surely your house must be one of the ones pictured. I can't believe it!"

Harriet looks at me and says, "You may come and stay in this room anytime you want."

Harriet closes the shutters and we go up to another floor and Harriet introduces me to Mary, an art student who lives in this self-contained room with skylights. Out the window I can see some church spires. Mary has easels and some artwork lying around. What a pleasant place to work. We head back down the many steps. The kitchen is calling to me. I must get back into that room. I sit down again at the table, look out the window and have some more tea. I do not want to leave.

Our time in Bruges seems to be flying by. Only one full day left. How sad. We've enjoyed meals at some of our favorite restaurants and we've given some of them our own special names, such as Blabbers and Rambo's! This time we decide to try a Spanish restaurant. I feel like paella with chicken but unfortunately there is no chicken and so it is monkfish and vegetables. Still, it is delicious.

On this lovely last evening, Ed and I walk and walk under a beautiful starlit sky with its almost-full moon. How can we be leaving tomorrow?

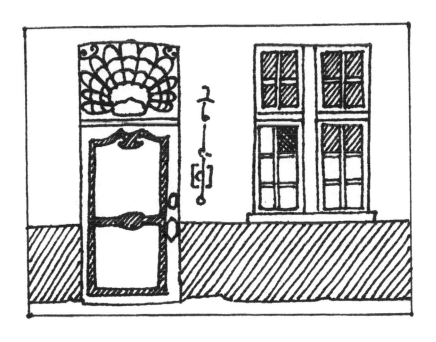

Chapter 8

The Beguinage - 1989

D ue to late planes and trains, I don't arrive in Bruges until 7:40 pm and it is pouring rain. My raincoat and umbrella are packed and I have on a white linen-cotton jacket! I hail a taxi and once again I am let off at the gate of the Beguinage and must walk in with my two suitcases. A warm welcome from Sister Mechtilde, who is just on her way to church, more than makes up for the struggle getting here. Then it is off to see Lislie who treats me to yogurt and freshly squeezed orange juice. It is great to see her and it doesn't even feel as if I had been away! She invites me to go with her to a Canal Festival tomorrow night.

We only visit briefly as I must settle in at the Beguinage. This time, I'm back in my very first room. Now I know that I prefer the one beside it but this one is nice for writing and being able to glance out the window. On my desk, I see a small blue jug filled with pink geraniums, a small box of chocolates, and a welcoming note from Lislie. What a lovely surprise!

The next morning I take a peaceful hour-long walk. It is cool but there is no rain. I visit briefly with Lislie in the afternoon and learn that the Canal Festival starts at eight thirty and will go on for hours. I realize that I'll need to talk with Sister Mechtilde about getting into the Beguinage well after ten o'clock!

Sure enough, Sister Mechtilde explains everything and now I know the secret! I can stay out with Lislie as late as I want. I can now also walk late in the courtyard. Every year, I learn something new!

I feel very relaxed. Time seems to go quickly when I live in the moment and I don't waste energy worrying about the future. I feel no pressure to be "doing" or "planning".

What I saw of the Canal Festival was delightful but due to rain, much of it was cancelled. What a lot of umbrellas and walking and standing. I don't know how Lislie does it! However, before heading home, we take some refreshments at a café called the Cat. In this lovely retreat from the rain, I sip on red wine while Lislie has a warmed, red wine. The drinks come with a nice presentation of dry, crisp, thin slices of toast and little crackers. I'm back to the Beguinage at 11:30 pm and I find it easy to open the door. All is dark and quiet. Thank goodness I always carry my little flashlight!

Next morning after a great sleep, I notice that it's a very dull looking day. But the clouds are moving and I can see a bit of blue sky. How I would love to see some sun. As always there is a standing invitation to visit Lislie, and if it is raining, she suggests that I come for the whole day.

"You don't want to be stuck in that little cell of a room."

She doesn't really listen to me when I tell her it's no problem! People going to Church this morning are going to get very wet. I can do nothing about the weather so I'll just forget about it! I feel very relaxed, almost as if I've never been away as I'm settling in so easily.

At breakfast, a visiting sister from Wales asks me to walk with her tonight to see the lights of Bruges. We leave at eight thirty. She is quite a slow walker and we are in three heavy rain showers. What am I doing? Off two nights in a row with much older women in pouring rainstorms!

I'm happy to be back at the Beguinage and decide to have a small bath tonight although I feel guilty if I use too much water. Why? I pay for each bath, twenty francs. So I'll just sink in and enjoy the bath in the large tub.

A few evenings later, I attend a presentation of medieval dancing with Lislie. It is held in the Belfry, a great setting complete with a bird flying around the stage! It is an excellent performance with dancing, costumes, music, and lots of great energy. I enjoy it immensely.

When we arrive back at the Beguinage, Lislie says,

"If you would like, I've arranged for us to go sightseeing in Ghent tomorrow. A couple that I know will pick us up at ten tomorrow morning."

"Sounds great! I'll be at your place at ten. Thanks for a great evening. See you tomorrow."

The next morning, Lislie introduces me to Odette and to her husband Georges, who projects a wonderful liveliness. I like them both. Little did I realize then that they would take Ed and me on so many car trips exploring outside of Bruges. Each time Ed and I came to Bruges, they would have something planned. Once in Oostende we walked the lovely sandy beach by the North Sea. We were at Ypres, site of many very bloody battles in the First World War. On the east side of the town there is an arched war memorial, the

Menin Gate, and each evening a group of buglers perform a Last Post Ceremony, which is very moving.

There were many more excursions filled with lots of laughter and fun. Ed and Georges enjoyed talking with each other as they shared the same sense of humor. Returning from the trips, I always felt excited as we drove over one of the bridges and entered Bruges once more.

This first time meeting Odette and Georges, I am on my own, staying at the Beguinage. Odette says that she would like to take me to her home and we arrange to meet at one of the bridges near the Beguinage the next day.

"Life is easy," says Odette as she stands on a small bridge over the canal. Seeing her bright yellow top, her sparkling deep brown eyes, I think, "butterfly" as she is so like one, such a free spirit. I love the energy that emanates from her.

"Oh Odette, how incredible that you say to me that life is easy! It is just what I needed to hear. Shortly before I left Canada, I was talking to one of my friends and she said to me, "Margaret, you always tend to think of things as being hard. Perhaps you need to change your thinking and think "easy." And here I come to Bruges and meet you and you tell me that life is easy. Amazing!"

Odette just laughs and we continue down the cobblestone streets, past the joined brick buildings and the little bakery with a window full of small tarts topped with fresh raspberries, tortes with kiwi and pineapple slices, apricots and little clusters of red berries, apple tarts and meringues. My mouth waters especially for the raspberry tarts. We continue on past a chocolate shop where the smell of chocolate wafts out into the street. Their display is exquisite with chocolates, light, dark and white, plus marzipan in the shape of lemons, oranges, peaches, bananas, apples, and even carrots. People jostle past us, mostly tourists carrying open maps and looking bewildered. They sometimes ask and I often can direct them and when I do, I feel like I belong in this medieval city.

Odette and I leave the shops and enter a residential street. The houses are flush with the streets. I used to think that it was sad that they didn't have yards, grass and trees but I now know that flowers, trees and some grass are at the back of the houses. We enter Odette's home and go through a small hall with a table at one side with some beeswax candles in holders and then through a glass door into the dining room. There is a long dining table, a piano, lovely oil paintings of flowers, very open flowing arrangements, nothing at all set and precise about the pictures.

"My mother painted those and she didn't start painting until she was sixty-eight and she has won prizes for her painting."

"I like her work, tell me more about her."

"Well, she is a very beautiful woman and when she was in her early twenties, she and her mother attended a parade in her town. They moved past people to get into the front row. In one of the beautiful horse-drawn carriages there was a young Belgian prince and as the carriage slowly passed by, the prince just stared and stared at my mother and continued staring as he went past. Mother felt embarrassed and hurried away.

Now to move far ahead to a year or so after my mother had started painting at sixty-eight and she won a prize for her work and, guess what? The prince was there to present the prizes! When my mother's name was announced, she walked up to the prince and he looked at her intensely and said, "It's you. I remember seeing you in the town of Oostende. I have never forgotten your face."

"What an experience, just imagine after all those years!"

We walk through the compact kitchen and out a glass door into a small, enclosed courtyard, framed on two sides by the house, and by faded brick walls on the other two sides. There is a wrought iron table and chairs. Vines cover some of the brick walls and there are a few small trees and roses blooming. There is a tall clay statue, made by Odette, of a monk-like figure with an open hand held up close to his face and a small bird perched in his hand.

"I like that Odette. It is as if the monk is saying, "Be free, little bird, fly away."

I look at Odette and say with a laugh, "Or else, I know what he could be saying, "Life is easy!"

Chapter 9

A Special Treat

Another day and I seem to have my very peaceful Bruges feeling back. I loved walking today noticing the trees, the beauty all around. On my way back, I go into the Beguine Museum house. I love the outside cloister by the well. How peaceful it is and how lovely it is to just be here, without even planning it. That is the way I like my days to unfold but today I'm looking forward to a visit with Harriet.

I pull the huge oak door of the Beguinage shut then follow the path across the lawn, going out the main entrance. I stop and watch a canal boat loaded with tourists going under the bridge. A group of swans is gently gliding along behind their leader. They look so majestic in their water-world but the minute they are on land, they lose their elegance, that certain something that sets them apart. When humans move out of their comfort zone, do they too lose something?

On past the outdoor café tables, a bakery with delicious looking round loaves of bread, all crusty-brown and topped with grains, a small lace shop, and the entrance to a hotel, I then turn left and continue on to Harriet's house. I look at my watch. Tea is at four and it's five after. I've made good time walking from the Beguinage. I ring the bell and see through the glass window in her dark blue door that Harriet is coming down the hall from her kitchen. She greets me with a hug. On the table just inside the door I notice a bouquet of yellow freesias, and then I am off to sit in my favorite place at her kitchen table with a view of the canal and a distant church spire.

"Oh, Harriet, it smells so delicious in here!"

"It's the apple tart. I made it especially for you." She also makes my favorite tea, mango.

"When does Ed arrive?"

"In three days. The time has gone by so quickly. I thought that I would get more meditative time for myself. Lislie has wanted me to visit with her often and she has been teaching me some piano. I've picked up fruit for her from the market and a skirt from the seamstress. I've enjoyed Lislie but it has been busy.

"Yes, Lislie can be demanding at times!"

Harriet gives me another piece of apple tart. I glance out the window as a canal boat goes past. The driver waves at Harriet and all the tourists in the boat look up at the window. I smile and hope that they think that I live here!

"I have a special treat for you today. I'll take you to the home of my friend Therese. She's away for a few days and I have to feed her cat."

We finish our tea and I rather reluctantly leave her cozy kitchen. At Harriet's front door, we turn left, then walking along the cobblestones we make a few more turns and very soon arrive at a large brown door. Harriet inserts the key and we enter a spacious front hall. She opens another door and we go through into the kitchen where she calls,

"Gateau, Gateau!" Suddenly through the dining room and into the kitchen comes a large grey cat with deep green eyes. He brushes against Harriet's legs and she bends down to pat him, talking softly to him. As soon as she has filled his empty dish with cat food, Gateau begins to eat immediately.

"Now, for what I really want to show you! Follow me," says Harriet as she leaves the kitchen.

We go through the dining room, past a beautiful wood table, and then into another large area with a stairway going upstairs on one side and an entrance to a large living room with a fireplace on the other. Also in this large hall is a door to the outside. Harriet pushes open this door and we are instantly in a medieval garden enclosed with brick walls. I can hear the canal boats going past. I can see the top of the Gruuthuse Museum and the much higher steeple of the Church of Our Lady.

"Harriet, how delightful to be in here! I never knew about this. How often I've passed so close by walking on that little bridge over the canal. I feel so caught up in the beauty and the surprise of it all!"

Harriet is beaming at me. "I knew that you would appreciate it. This building in the back of the garden is a house that has been furnished in an authentic medieval way. I'll take you in there, too."

"To whom does this belong?"

"It belongs to a Count in Brussels and sometimes some of his family or friends come and stay in the medieval house. There has even been a film made here! My friend takes care of it for them."

"Let's go inside. I can't wait to see it!"

Harriet pulls some keys out of her pocket. "Just wait until I find the right key."

It is rather dim in the first room. There is a large long table to the left and to the right there is an open hearth with cooking pots. Close by is a shelf filled with books. I'm immediately drawn to them. They are somewhat dusty and very old. None are in English but I open the pages and look at them. I would love to own one, such ancient books made at a time when Indians still were hunting buffalo in my country. On the table are some thick green glasses with little pointed projections all around them. I pick one up and examine it. Harriet says,

"Do you know why they were made this way?"

"No, I thought it was just a design. Do you mean there is a reason for it?"

"Yes, they were made this way so that a knight wouldn't have to remove his mail glove in order to drink out of the glass. Without the pointed projections, the glass would slip out of his hands!"

"How clever!"

We leave that room, go past a stairway leading to a second story, and enter into a smaller room. It reminds me of a small study. There is a desk covered by a green cloth, a wooden bookstand holding an open book, and a high-backed wooden desk chair embellished with some carving.

Sitting beside the desk is a large stuffed lion. I stare at the chair, at the desk, and the lion and I'm certain that I've seen something almost like this before. But where or when, I don't know. Behind the desk are shelves with small stacks of books, and something that looks like a beaker with a tall thin neck. Green curtains hang to each side and can be pulled across the shelves.

"Harriet, this looks familiar to me. Why is there a lion here?"

"This room is designed according to a painting of St. Jerome, and his symbol was always the lion. Of course, in the original painting, St. Jerome was seated at the desk. The painter was Jan van Eyck and we have two of his paintings here in the Groeninge Museum. One is a religious painting and the other one is of his wife, Margaret!"

"How interesting that her name was Margaret! In what year was it painted?"

"It was in the 1400s. I think that the date was 1439."

We leave this room and go upstairs and into the two bedrooms. In one there is a remarkably elaborate bed with four high bedposts topped with a canopy.

"One of the scenes in the film was shot in this bedroom."

"I would love to see this film."

"It was only a small production and it wouldn't have been released internationally. It was done in Flemish."

I look at my watch. "It is time I left as the gates at the Beguinage will soon be closing. I would love to have Ed see this. Do you think that would be possible?"

"Therese will be back by then so I'll ask her and if she knows that you're truly interested, I'm sure that she'll let you come."

Ed does get to see the exquisite medieval house, and I get to see it again too! Once we're inside, I stand and look at the desk and the lion and try to remember what it reminds me of or where I've seen it. It doesn't trigger anything with Ed.

Shortly after we arrive home from our Bruges trip, I decide to look for some art pictures and I find an envelope of them tucked away in my cedar chest. When the children were young, I had clipped pictures that appealed to me out of art brochures and magazines and I put them up on a bulletin board in the kitchen. I wanted to expose the children to some art.

I search through the envelope of pictures, remembering the ones that I really liked and some of the children's favorites. Suddenly I find the one with the lion! It is just like the setting in the medieval house except that in this picture, St. Jerome is seated at the desk looking at a book on the bookstand. It seems amazing that this picture drew me to cut it out and keep it for over twenty years! Who was this St. Jerome? I bet my Catholic friends would know. I decide to look in my books and see what I can find out about him. I read about his life, his time spent in the desert, his interest in learning, and I find something about the lion. Jerome took a thorn out of a lion's paw and the lion became his devoted companion! I'm also amazed to learn that September 30 is St. Jerome's feast day, the day after my birthday. How extraordinary! I'm constantly amazed at my "tie-ins" with Bruges. I'm drawn to something and I keep it and then many years later, I find there is a connection to it in Bruges! It is as if I always knew that I would go there. But just seeing the picture—it doesn't say "Bruges." It is always much more subtle. As I write about this, I feel the excitement rising inside me. Dear Bruges, I do love you and all the mystery that keeps unfolding for me there, and it hasn't ended yet.

A balance. That is what I'm always striving for. It should be easy for one who is a Libra, whose symbol is the scale. I have a desire to read about medieval times, find out more about the Beguines, about the life of women and the conditions that existed at that time. Immerse myself. Write about that time that at one level I seem instinctively to know about. Go back, go way back… What was my name then? Margaret comes to mind. That is my name now, and as I have discovered, there are many Margarets in Flemish history.

But I've jumped ahead and there is more to tell regarding our visit with Harriet's friend, Therese. She has a room in her house where Ed and I can stay the next year when we come to Bruges. We agree that we would love to stay and will pay her for bed and breakfast. What serendipity! It seems that we have never really had to plan for where we will stay the next year. It seems before one door closes, another has already opened, which is very fortunate as, in a few years, Adrian will sell his hotel and then we would have had to search for another place.

Chapter 10

Staying at Therese's Home - September 1990 and 1991

We arrived yesterday in the late afternoon and it was first to Harriet's house for mango tea and her very thin pancakes with their little dusting of brown sugar... delicious! Then it's off to Therese's house.

Our lovely room is on the second floor and it has a large bed, TV, couch, and a table to sit at to write or to eat. Nearby is a bathroom furnished with a long bathtub. We'll have our breakfast downstairs in the sitting room at nine where we will sit at a table by a group of windows overlooking the canal. I am thrilled as our upstairs window also looks out on the canal, the bridge, and the side and back of the church.

"How about going for a night-time walk?"

"Perfect," says Ed.

We stroll along a cobblestone street and over a bridge where we pause to look down at the canal, then off through a little alcove and along to an entrance way into the Burg. My Bruges feeling flows over me. It feels wonderful and I feel so content to be here.

The next morning at nine, we enjoy our breakfast of orange juice, a variety of buns, cheese and meats, with tea for me and coffee for Ed, all the while sitting at the table by the windows and watching the canal boats going past. We chat briefly with Therese, and then she puts on some music and leaves us to relax and eat and eat.

"Ed, with breakfasts like this, we won't even need lunch!"

"This coffee is delicious. Oh look, here comes a canal boat loaded with people."

"That is what we may be doing tonight as Harriet is going to try and set up an evening boat ride for us."

Fuelled by our ample breakfast we walk for ages before popping in at Harriet's. She confirms the evening canal ride. "Come around eight thirty and we'll go from here." And then we are off again exploring the streets of Bruges. This time we decide to walk a little farther and look for the Buffalo Bridge. During one of our first visits to Bruges, Ed and I learned that the Canadians are well liked in this city. It was the Canadian troops who liberated Bruges in the Second World War on September 12, 1944. One of the bridges, named the Buffalo Bridge, has two buffalo/bison at one end memorializing the troops of the Royal Winnipeg Rifles and the Regina Rifles. In the end, we found that the bridge was too far for us to reach on foot so we didn't arrive there that day. We'll definitely check it out another time.

That evening on our way to Harriet's I remark,

"Ed, how special for us to be going in the evening as usually the boats just tour during the day unless some arrangement is made by a group."

I have on a sweater and a cardigan and Harriet lends me her lovely fine wool stole, a deep blue and so cozy. I love how it looks and feels on me and it is just perfect for tonight. On the boat ride, it is exciting to glide past Harriet's house and also Therese's. The trees look so lovely in the evening light.

Afterwards, Harriet, Ed and I go for cappuccinos. What a lovely ending to a great night!

The trip is starting to seem so short, partly because I didn't arrive earlier and stay at the Beguinage. I feel the need to take more time for peaceful walks and sitting quietly by the water. But this time seems to be a people holiday including drives out of Bruges and into the countryside. Yesterday, Georges and Odette drove us to Sluis, a very vibrant Dutch town. We explored the historical sites, and the bustling streets and shops, before relaxing with tea, coffee and waffles.

We feel very comfortable in our room by the medieval garden and plan to stay here next year. Edmonton seems so very far away as I feel so "at home" here in Bruges. I'm feeling positive and have my quiet center intact. Something special happens for me when I sit in Harriet's kitchen. Yesterday, Harriet told me that I looked very happy. I always seem to feel such an excitement in that house! Right now, church bells are ringing and the sound resonates deep within me. How I wish I could feel this vibrancy more often when I am in Edmonton.

We've been in Bruges now for ten days and in a few more days we'll be leaving. No, no, no! On September 24, Harriet comes to the train station with us, stands on the platform and waves to us until we can no longer see her. The train moves through the Belgian countryside, ever further away from Bruges. I feel tears beginning to fall. I look at Ed.

"Why do I always get tears? I had a lovely time." Ed just smiles and pats my hand.

September 1991

I'll have seven days at the Beguinage and then Ed and I will stay at Therese's for ten days.

When I arrive at the Beguinage, I am given a small room facing out to the front, my first time in a front room. One advantage to this is that it will be cooler later in the day. It was very hot in Amsterdam and on the train. Here too in Bruges it feels like the middle of summer. It is nice looking out the window at the lawn and trees, and there are no tourists. But they will be back tomorrow morning! Each night at six thirty, the doors of the two stone gates, separating the Beguinage from the rest of the town, swing shut and are locked.

This room doesn't have hot water! I've been lucky the other years to have a sink with hot and cold running water, but then Sister Mechtilde was in charge. I do have a comfortable chair though! I'm going to enjoy this chair, much better to sit in than a straight-backed desk chair. There is a note and chocolates from Lislie on the desk.

Even though I have had a good sleep, I wake up with sore eyes. That's probably from the smoke on the plane. Why are people allowed to smoke on planes? Nine hours of that is just too much. But, just let that go… I'm in Bruges again!

It is Lislie's birthday today. It is good to see her again, vibrant as ever at 84. I feel that she'll be going strong for a number of years! Today, along with Harriet, Joleen and a few other friends, we celebrate with delicious cupcakes, tarts, coffee and tea.

Back from Lislie's, I sit in the garden behind the Beguinage. It is a beautiful warm day. The Sister who is now in charge comes to sit beside me.

"Margaret, I'll move you to Room 15 if you like."

"Thanks but I'm unpacked and settled in so I'll just stay where I am. I want to let you know that I won't be here for supper on Saturday and will come back later in the evening."

"That will be alright. You'll just have to be very quiet."

Lislie is always arranging things and they are always so interesting and enjoyable. This time I have a small meal with her before we are to be picked up and driven to a concert by her gentleman friend, Noel. The drive takes three quarters of an hour to the town of Veurne where the concert is being held in its ancient gothic church. Before the concert, I have tea, Lislie has coffee, and Noel has a beer.

The concert, featuring a string ensemble from Brussels, is wonderful and the music brings me to tears. The acoustics are excellent especially in the piece by Puccini. Afterwards, at the champagne reception we nibble on pate spread on little rounds of bread, garnished with parsley, all so appealing and delicious too. Just before I leave Lislie, I say,

"You've introduced me to some very interesting people, especially Harriet and Odette." She looks at me and says,

"Well, I'm just a bridge for you."

Later in the evening I am thankful that I am able to use the key correctly to get back into the Beguinage. I think about my lovely evening as I quietly tiptoe up the stairs and down the hall to my bedroom.

Next morning, the sun is shining and church bells are ringing. There are not too many people around and as I walk I realize that I'm a vessel slowly being refilled and replenished. So much replenishment of my soul has to take place and each day I feel it happening. Today is my fifth full day here! It has gone by very quickly and yet in another way I feel that I have always been here. What was it like for medieval women? I must immerse myself in this question, write about that time that at one level I seem to know so much about. Go back, go way back...

> *I hurry down the dark cobblestone streets and into my home. Mother is in the kitchen stirring a large pot of soup. It smells so good on this damp, chilly night. Mother looks tired. I take the soupspoon from her and say,*
> *"Sit down for a while. I'll stir this."*
> *Her tired face looks grateful as she sits on a chair on the other side of the stove. Father comes in rubbing his hands together.*
> *"It is cold out there and the church seems even colder. My fingers were so cold that I could hardly play."*
> *With a sigh, he sits down at the table and buries his head in his arms. I feel the need to go*

back outside. I could walk to my favorite bridge and stand and look at the beautiful reflections in the water. That is always so calming and inspiring for me. I'm sure neither Father nor Mother notice the beauty anymore. But I stay and stir the soup and chatter about my day, hoping to lift them out of their gloom. It doesn't seem to help. I take some bowls out of the cupboard, ladle out the soup and place the bowls on the table next to the round loaf of bread, sitting on the breadboard, with a knife to one side. I never slice the bread as everyone says that I don't cut straight but cause a big slant on the loaf. What does it matter? But it does.

This time I leave the Beguinage the day before Ed is to arrive. Therese has left a key with me as she won't be in until late afternoon. I unpack before my walk in the medieval garden. I so love to walk and sit in this garden. When Therese arrives she finds me in the garden, and she exclaims,

"Oh, you look so young and so beautiful."

What a marvelous lift to my soul!

Now that I am in my room in Therese's house, it feels so good to have more space. I just don't know if I'll be going back to the Beguinage again. I'm not quite ready to give that up as I need that quiet space upon my arrival and the peacefulness it gives my soul. But it is not quite the same for me now that Sister Mechtilde is no longer in charge.

Next morning I go downstairs to a delicious breakfast. There are melon balls, green and purple grapes, pineapple chunks, breads, cheeses, and tea. Therese has put on some classical music... how lovely. I look out the window and see two swans swimming down the canal. One is behind the other and seemingly moving to the classical music! Then I notice a group of art students arrive and take up their drawing positions along the side of the building, presumably to draw the bridge over the canal. It looks like a lovely day. I want to buy stamps, go to the market, have a visit with Lislie and get back here for some peaceful time to myself before Ed arrives in the afternoon.

Of course, when Ed arrives, it is great to see him and we hug and kiss. Later, over dinner at Rambo's we enjoy delicious food and a relaxed "catch-up" time.

Time seems to be passing very quickly and I am aware of sometimes feeling sad and closed to Bruges. Why? I am walking the streets, seeing the canals but not feeling wholly here, right here in this moment. How do I break through? I know that I can't and that I must be patient and hope that it will just happen. Perhaps I need to be in Harriet's kitchen where I always feel so good.

The days go by, only a few more until we leave. I wake up after a good sleep and I can see a deep blue sky through our leaded glass windows. After a delicious breakfast, I go for a walk by myself and as I walk and hear the sound of church bells, some of my deep fulfilling Bruges feeling starts to come back.

I hurry along the cobblestone street and see a man, about forty, coming towards me. He stops and asks me something in stilted Flemish. I say, "I speak English," and he exclaims, "I thought you lived here!"

"No, but I can probably help you."

"Do you know the way to the Burg?"

"Yes, you just go through this walkway with shops on each side and at the end you'll reach the Burg." I point out the direction to him and he smiles and thanks me. I continue my walk and his words run through my head… "I thought you lived here." What a thrill! I love it when people think that I live here and ask me for directions. This is the third time that I've been asked in the past two weeks!

On our last night, Ed and I go to Harriet's for dinner. She is going to cook rabbit! I have never eaten it before but Ed has when he was a young boy growing up on a farm. As soon as we enter Harriet's home, I notice that it smells like chicken cooking - but no, it is rabbit! The meal is delicious but I still can't believe that I ate rabbit!

Harriet tells us we are invited to Therese's for tea and goodies. When we arrive, we are surprised to see that we will have our "dessert" in the medieval house. There are candles lit and windows open to the night view of the church and the medieval garden. What a very special last night in Bruges!

Chapter 11

A Sad Return from
Bruges - 1991

We arrive back home on Saturday, September 21 to a busy week. Ed has an Engineering Reunion dinner for that Friday. Also that weekend, our daughter Debbie will be driving up from Calgary, and our daughter Barbara and her husband, Stephen and their puppy, will join together with our Edmonton daughter Linda, to celebrate my birthday, which is on September 29. But this time, we'll celebrate it on the 28th as they'll be returning to Calgary the next day.

On the night of the 23rd, I dream that I'm in bed with Ed and I move closer into his arms. He is almost asleep and so am I. All of a sudden, I am under the covers and his arm is too heavy on me. I struggle to get out and try to call out, "Let go---I can't breathe!" As I struggle, he says, "Just relax," but I panic and struggle eventually shooting out of the covers and gasping for breath. At this point, I wake up and Ed says, "You must have been having a bad dream." I tell him about it and realize that I was dreaming and he says, "I didn't know whether to wake you as you were thrashing around and making low sounds."

"It was terrible. I would call it a nightmare! I don't know if I can go back to sleep."

"Let me hold you. Cuddle into me."

I snuggle into him, close my eyes and try to replace the frightening images with soft, gentle caring ones.

I belonged to a dream group for years and usually write down my dreams and title them. Rarely have I had a nightmare but this certainly was one and I title it, "Stifled and Smothered." What could it mean?

We celebrate my birthday on the 28th and the next day, on my real birthday, Ed goes golfing early in the morning. Debbie is up to hug him and say goodbye. A short time later, Barbara and Stephen leave and Debbie and I go to the ravine for a walk before she leaves.

It is autumn in Edmonton and the leaves are changing color and many are starting to fall. We walk and walk and then we follow a new path and on and on we go until eventually, I say,

"Don't you think it is time that we turn back? We've come a long way."

"Oh, Mom, don't you always want to know what's just around the corner?"

I think to myself—yes, that's my daughter, always curious and wanting to explore.

"Well, Debbie, sometimes I do and sometimes I don't want to know."

We go a little further before heading back. Along the way we sit down on a log, continue our conversation, just enjoying being there in each other's company. Then off we go again on this lovely September day, my birthday. Little did I know it would be our last walk, our last time to explore, and our last time together. In less than twenty-four hours,

Debbie is dead, the final diagnosis being acute leukemia. She died on September 30ᵗʰ, the day after my birthday.

We contacted our son Philip. He is deeply shocked and makes travel arrangements to come to Edmonton. Much grieving, many letters, phone calls, visits… it was a sudden death and people could not believe it. Debbie loved life and celebrated it.

In my life, I've experienced the sudden deaths of my grandma and my dad and I never felt that I truly dealt with them. But since then, I've volunteered at the Cross Cancer Institute and talked with patients who were facing death. I also attended an excellent talk by Dr. Elizabeth Kübler-Ross, the author of "On Death and Dying," and I learned a great deal. I vow to myself that I won't go over or under this grief, but through it.

In November 1988, I started my early morning journal writing. I'm not a morning person and so I am amazed that I continued to journal every morning for the next twenty-five years. In 1991, it helped me to deal with the grief of Debbie's death.

In May and early June of 1991, I taught a course on Journal Writing. I had peonies just starting to bloom in my garden and I took a large fragrant bouquet to each class. I enjoyed the teaching and had another class set up for October but I cancelled it as Debbie had only just died. Later in June, I attended my first freefall writing workshop at Doe Bay on Orcas Island, Washington. I learned an approach to writing that seemed to be right for me! In November, a few months after Debbie's death, I attended my second freefall writing workshop, this time in La Push, Washington. I agonized over whether I should go so soon after my daughter's death but I had already registered and I wondered if it might help me in more ways than one.

Ed and I drove to this quiet seaside village at the northernmost point of Washington's Pacific Coast beaches. It was comforting with just the two of us, and the driving and driving. When we arrived we said our good-byes and then for the duration of the workshop, Ed visited with a friend in Seattle.

Wind, movement, waves crashing, branches trembling, birds soaring… can nothing just *be?* But, life is not static. If it is, you're dead. In La Push, while the turbulent, pounding waves crashed onto the shore, I screamed and roared and released some of my grief. I wrote about Debbie's birth, a 10-pound, 23-inch baby! How did I carry all this inside me?

Once we are back at home, Ed raked leaves and did manual things. I talked to close friends and also wrote about Debbie's death. We each worked through our grief in our own ways.

Months go by and a friend asked me why I didn't go to Bruges, as it seemed to be such a healing place for me. I felt as if a light had gone on. Ed and I had planned to go there in the fall. I talked with him and he thought that I should definitely go and he suggested June. I thought that would be perfect as it would be nine months after Debbie's death and also, June was her birthday month. We also decide that we'll go in October. How special, as I'll be in Bruges twice in one year!

Our friends in Bruges were devastated to learn about Debbie's death. I phone Harriet to see if I can stay with her. She is happy to have me. I decide to stay four days at the Beguinage to get over jet lag and to immerse myself in its solitude. Then I will go to Harriet's.

Chapter 12

Taking My Grief to
Bruges - June 1992

I arrive in Bruges on Friday and settle into the Beguinage, then go for a quick walk before the evening meal. Once again I see a large rabbit in the grass near where Ed and I always meet. I've seen rabbits before in this area and have taken pictures of them. When I showed one to Lislie, she was amazed and said, "We never see rabbits here! May I have a copy of that picture?" Back in my room, I notice that I have a note from Harriet saying that she'll pick me up at 1:30 on Monday and her wish that I have peaceful days in the Beguinage. Also there are lovely chocolates from Lislie and in her note I learn that she'll be away in The Hague for a few days for some dental treatment.

It feels good to be here, almost immediately calming. What is it about Bruges that can do this to me?

The next day I go for an afternoon walk but I can't seem to lose myself the way I did yesterday.

Searching

Bruges, where are you?
Where do I search
To find you?
Will it no longer come to flame?
Has it given its all?

I howl – cry into the night
Do not desert me!
I need that peaceful surge
That feeling of peace

I open the door and go out once more to search.
May the Gods be with me.

I have enjoyed seeing all the baby ducks with their protective mothers, but today I have thoughts of Debbie and the void in our family. I miss her so much. When will this ache diminish? I wish that I had brought more books to study and learn from but perhaps I need to turn inwards to self and just be still.

Another day and just after the noon meal, Sister Monica tells me that I have a visitor in the library. It is a friend of Lislie's who tells me that Lislie won't be returning until next week as she is having extensive dental work done. She gives me the key to Lislie's house and now I'll be able to go there for a change of scenery. For me this will mean lots of quiet, uninterrupted time and that must be what I need. I have a comfortable tiredness and no desire to meet with people. I need rest and space before I go to Harriet's in just two-and-a-half days.

Next morning, it is pouring rain and I decide to postpone my walk until the afternoon. When I ask Sister Mary Ann about Sister Mechtilde, she takes me to see her. Sister Mechtilde looks pale and much older but her spark is certainly still there! She knows about Debbie and is very comforting to me. The tears are coming. People do say, "You will be reunited with her again." That is small comfort to me. She died much too young. Oh Debbie, I miss you so much!

I walk, sit and watch baby ducks, such young curious life. I need to let go, let myself just "be." I continue to walk and walk. Did I live here in a past life? Did I walk on these cobblestones? Who was I? What did I do? I must have been happy because I can feel so happy here, so alive, so calm and peaceful.

Harriet picks me up from the Beguinage and drives me to her home. We have tea and talk for hours. When Harriet has gone shopping, I unpack. Next to my bedroom there is a warm, inviting bathroom with a big bathtub, and there is a chair by the window in the bedroom. Sitting there, I can hear church bells and the sound of horse's hooves on cobblestones. I love it.

Harriet returns and after our light supper, she asks,

"Would you like to go for a night-time walk?"

Part of me thinks—no, I'm tired, but then another voice comes and says, "Why not? You like to walk and it'll be your first evening walk in Bruges." So, I answer, "yes." I'm wearing my blue pants, a pink sweater, and I put my silk jacket over top and zip it up. I slip my glasses into my open side pocket. We walk up to the corner and debate which way to go.

"I know where we'll go." says Harriet.

We cross the street, walk a short way, and then Harriet turns into a very narrow cobblestone alley. We're talking and hurrying along when all of a sudden, I trip and down I go skidding the left side of my face along the cobblestones.

I am momentarily stunned and shaken but I sit up, then stand and say,

"I'm alright."

Harriet takes one look at me and exclaims, "We're going home."

I feel wetness on my cheek and put a tissue over it as we hurry back to Harriet's. When I look in her hall mirror I see that I have a red gaping cut, just below my left eyebrow, which is bleeding, and my cheek is skinned.

Harriet washes my wounds, puts on some creams and I hold an ice pack to my face to reduce the swelling. She asks,

"Should I call a doctor?"

"I don't know. Maybe it requires stitches."

"I'll call my friend Mary Ann to come and have a look. She is a nurse."

But when she calls there is no answer, so she calls the doctor. His line is busy so she tries Mary Ann again. This time she is home and will come right away.

Mary Ann is gentle and kind as she examines me and notes that the cut is not deep enough for stitches. She asks me how my cheek feels, as maybe it needs to be x-rayed. I don't feel that anything is broken. Mary Ann cleans the cut and paints it with some kind of healing red liquid. After she has left I attempt to drink a glass of water but I can only do so by looking in a mirror. The side of my lip, cheek, and nose is totally numb. I feel as if I've been at the dentist and it is frozen. Before I go to bed, Harriet puts a bandage over the cut to stop the oozing blood.

Sleep simply will not come. My right ear is thumping and static-like. I start to wonder about the numbness and why I have it. Is it because it's swollen or have I hurt a nerve that gives feeling to that side of my face? Eventually I fall asleep but awake suddenly and am startled to see Harriet standing by the bed looking at me! She had just wanted to check and see how I was so I drift back to sleep.

The next morning at breakfast, Harriet makes me a soft milk pudding that is easy to eat and bread with the crusts cut off. I can eat a little better though the numbness is still there. Afterwards I have a bath and go back to bed for a couple of hours. It is close to one when I finally get up. As I walk down the stairs, I smell something delicious. Harriet has made leek soup. That and more soft bread are quite nourishing and so comforting.

Mary Ann comes again. She takes off the taped bandage, cleans the cut and remarks that it looks good. My eye is puffy and swollen as is my cheek under my eye. I'll not be going out today, nor do I want to. I feel so much better after my morning sleep. I will survive. I'm so thankful that I'm here in Harriet's house.

While I rest, thoughts invade my tranquility. Why did I fall? It seems unbelievable and also that it happened on a Monday, as did Debbie's death. I fell on my left side, the feminine side. I need to nurture myself more and, I conclude, I'm here in Bruges to do just that.

Wednesday, two days since my fall, and last night I had a sound sleep but my eye is even more swollen. Today, Odette and Georges are taking me out for a drive and lunch outside of Bruges. They are very shocked when they see my face, so bruised and swollen. At a restaurant in Damme and then during an enjoyable walk through trees, we talk about Debbie's death and the death of Odette's mother, who died close to Debbie's death date. It feels good to be outside and walking, talking and enjoying nature.

Thursday, and I plan to go walking but I don't feel as independent with my face looking like this. As I walk, I almost want to turn my damaged face away from others. But the words of a friend of mine, who was in a wheelchair, come back —"I teach others how I want them to treat me." So, I'll just hold my head up and walk proudly!

In the afternoon, Harriet drives me out of Bruges to her farm, which belonged to her grandparents. On the way, we stop at a farm for milk and eggs and then take some to an older lady. I am touched by this woman's warmth and good energy and her concern about my injury. At Harriet's farm, we pick white raspberries, which I've never had, and I find they taste delicious. We sit outside and relax in the warmth of the sun… just what I need, warmth and serenity to help with my healing.

That evening, we visit Therese and she gives me a warm greeting and expresses sympathy about Debbie. She is very comforting, understanding my grief, as she tells me that her sister died at age twenty-five. We enjoy a glass of sherry, much conversation and some laughter. It feels so good being back in her home and I tell her that Ed and I are looking forward to staying here when we come in October.

Friday, and this is my first evening walk with Harriet since my fall. It is ten o'clock. The sky is a deep blue and the reflections in the canal are clear and lovely on this windless night. Such peace! I really love the evenings.

Before bed, I look at my face and see that the bruises are taking on a yellowish tinge. Is my feeling starting to come back? I weep for myself without Debbie. I can't believe that her physical presence is no more in my life. I must carry on her zest, her love of life, her risk-taking and her positivity.

I miss Ed when I am walking. It just seems that he should be here. Always he has arrived after I've been here for some days on my own. We have strong ties to each other and now we have so much grief to go through, each in our own way.

The next day, I see that the scab on part of my nose is coming loose. Hurray! I've been here over a week and will be seeing Lislie for the first time tomorrow. Harriet is off to a funeral today and I go for a long walk, look in a bookstore and buy some mango tea to take home. I also walk on the cobblestones where I fell and I shake my head in disbelief. I arrive back at Harriet's to hear the phone ringing. It is Ed! It's great to talk with him and I tell him about my fall. At the end of our talk, he says,

"You'll have fun picking off your scabs!"

When I visit Lislie, we hug and it feels so good to see her again. She is looking well. Over coffee and pastries she asks me to tell her about Debbie. I tell her of Debbie's love of nature and adventure, from hikes to whitewater canoeing, about how she named everything near and dear to her: her car, her plants, and a large toy monkey called Darwin. I show her pictures of Debbie and talk about her sudden death. Lislie listens and is very consoling. We talk and talk. Later, when I ask her to play the piano, she plays some Heller and it is beautiful.

Another time, Lislie and I sit with Harriet outside on her deck by the canal, and enjoy Belgian pancakes, tea and a few other goodies. Together we talk and laugh and relax. It is lovely to have such warm and compassionate friends in Bruges. It helps me, in every way, as I continue to heal.

I'm getting down to my last few days in Bruges. Yesterday, I walked by the canal and then sat on a bench. All of a sudden, my Bruges feeling overwhelmed me. Tears came and then it seemed as if everything slipped into place. A quiet peacefulness entered my soul. I felt ready to return home and continue with my life yet knowing that there would always be a missing piece.

The big scab on my face just came off and my skin looks great. I am healing so quickly! I just need to lose the numbness and the last scab below the cut on my eyebrow. I can't believe that it is now my last day and I leave tomorrow to take the train to Amsterdam and then fly home the next day. But first I must go to the chocolate shop to buy some boxes of chocolates to take back home. The last part of my eye scab just came off. I'll have no scabs left by the time I leave! The visible outside scabs are gone but healing is still going on within.

The next morning, I have my last Bruges walk. I feel too well to leave! In the afternoon, Harriet takes me to the train and stands on the platform and waves and waves as the train moves down the tracks. I feel the tears falling down my cheeks.

On the flight home, a stop is made in Calgary. Barbara and Stephen come to see me before I board the Edmonton flight. Barbara looks at me and exclaims,

"Mom, I thought you said that you fell on your face!"

When I arrive home, Ed is also amazed at how good my face looks. I show him some photos Harriet took of my face, the morning after, a few more as my time there progressed, and then one on the day I left. I'm so glad that she chronicled this fall and my healing. She included a picture of a statue in Bruges of a woman who has fallen down on the side of her face! It is Niobe of Greek mythology, daughter of Tentalus, wife of King Amphion of Thebes. She is the prototype of the bereaved mother. She was weeping for her dead children and was turned into stone but her tears still flowed. I see the connection immediately and how it was that I go to Bruges in grief over my daughter's death and fall down on my face!!

I'm now back home and have no reflections on my trip other than it was healing and nurturing for me. What more could I ask? I didn't come fully to terms with Debbie's death but this is still in process and will continue to be. I realize that what I needed was body rest, as well as Harriet's loving care.

Many, many years after my fall on the cobblestones in 1992, it happened one winter that Harriet slipped and fell on the cobblestones too. Recently she said to me, "You and I have both kissed the cobblestones!" I look at her and say, "Yes, not just any cobblestones but the cobblestones of Bruges!

Chapter 13

Returning to Bruges for a Second Time in 1992

E d and I are back again in Bruges, and once again staying at Therese's home. It is incredible that I just left here three months ago! When we go for our morning walk, I'm so relieved that I feel confident walking on the cobblestones. We drop into Harriet's for a visit and she is very happy to see us. I'm elated that I didn't have to wait a year before I came back. It is so very special to be in Bruges twice in one year. With busy days, visiting with Lislie, then off with Odette and Georges to Oostende where we walk on the sand by the ocean, my Bruges feeling is starting to invade me! Yum, yum! Joy, joy!

It's my first Beguinage walk today and I recognize how different it is now in September than it was in June. Now all the leaves are off the poplar trees giving them a stark majesty. I love walking around and around the paths, one circular and two others that cross at angles. I walk very slowly, my head down and my arms lightly folded in front of me with my fingers almost touching my elbows. I sometimes put my arms by my sides but they are quickly drawn back into my first position. I am not conscious of others around me.

In the evening, we attend a medieval concert, another joyful experience, and afterwards we have a lovely stroll back to Therese's under an almost-full moon. I love being able to walk everywhere in this picturesque historic town. Tonight Ed is going to cook dinner for Harriet and Therese. He is busy preparing it in Therese's kitchen and says,

"Margaret, would you go out and buy some celery for me? Thought that I had everything, but not so."

I rush out to buy the celery and I'm fully into my Bruges feeling. I love the canals and yes, even the cobblestones and the old buildings, the pealing of bells and the trees, the magnificent trees, and walking amid all this. I love it. I love it!

Many years later, I visit a Borders bookstore in Phoenix that I like very much. The bookshelves are not all in straight rows and there are cosy chairs hidden away here and there among the many shelves of books. I can choose a book, settle into a chair and feel as if I have my own private space. There is a winding staircase to the second floor with more books and also there is a great coffee shop, open on one side, where people can sip their drinks, eat their snacks, and look down onto the main floor. I love to get a large glass of iced tea, which they really seem to know how to make, and sit at a table where I can look down on people and books. Through the windows in the end wall of the coffee shop, I can glance out at the sky or at the huge tree at the edge of the parking lot. Sunshine pours through these windows. After all, this is Phoenix.

Today, Barbara and I do not have much time to spend in the bookstore, so no iced tea, just time to glance at a few books. As I look over some of the newer releases on a big table near the front of the store, my eye is attracted to a picture of a tree and I pick up the book titled, "The Healing Energies of Trees." In it are beautiful pictures of trees. On the back cover I read, "Ancient myths and legends celebrate the powerful energies of trees—as a source of food, shelter, and the sacred life force itself." Barbara comes up to me and asks,

"Are you finding anything?"

"This book looks very interesting. You know how I love trees. Is it time to go?"

"Yes, it's after four."

"I'm going to buy this. I don't know anything about it but I just feel so drawn to it."

Back at Barb's I don't really have time to look at the book, as I'm busy immersing myself in the world of my two young grandsons. Once Ed and I are back home, I unpack and put the book downstairs beside the fireplace where I plan to have a cup of tea and browse through it. Several nights later, Ed goes up to bed before me. As he bends down to give me a quick kiss, I say,

"I'm going to stay here awhile and look at this book."

"Okay, see you in bed."

I had looked quickly in the bookstore and I thought that the author's name was Patricia, but now I see it is Patrice. I read a random paragraph inside and find he is talking about trees often being planted at the birth of a new era, such as in France after the revolution when sixty thousand trees of Liberty were planted, and also that Belgians planted trees to celebrate their independence in 1830. My heart quickens as it always does when I find a mention of Belgium.

I leap ahead to the part about discovering the energy field of a tree. I remember so vividly an ancient tree on the island of Molokai and how each time I passed it, I would reach up to a branch and hold on with my two hands and close my eyes until, eventually, I felt in contact with the tree and could feel its energy flow through my arms. I read more about the energy field and look at some of the pictures. The author assigns different qualities to trees such as the Birch, whose qualities are gentleness and reconciliation. Interesting!

I feel ready for bed but decide to read a bit about the author and I learn that he gives workshops worldwide. Then I see the addresses where he can be reached. One is in the United States but the other is in Bruges! I read it again and I can't believe it. I'm so excited and I just have to tell Ed. He is in bed and looks asleep, but I ask anyway,

"Are you awake?"

"I am now."

"I'm sorry to wake you but I'm so excited. Guess what?"

"What?"

"This book I was so drawn to in Borders was written by a man from Bruges. I can't believe it! Here, look at the Bruges address."

"That's amazing!"

"Yes, out of all the books in the store, I was drawn to this one. What is this Bruges connection? I'm going to check this out next time that I'm there. Odette may have heard of him. I don't know if I can get to sleep. I'm so excited! Wait till I tell Barbara about this."

I look at a few more pictures in the book before going to bed with my mind whirling with yet another Bruges connection. But then, as I think about how much I love books, I am reminded of another Bruges connection! William Caxton of England settled in Bruges in 1441. Another Margaret in the history of Bruges was Margaret of York, who married Charles the Bold in Bruges in 1468. She later hired Caxton as her secretary and in 1472 she encouraged him to go to Cologne to learn about printing, something Caxton was very interested in. When he returned to Bruges with his printed manuscript, he presented it to Margaret of York. Using his new technology, he set up a printing press in Bruges and printed the first book in English! Shortly after that, he returned to England and set up a printing press and then in 1477, he published the first book printed in England.

Enough of remembrances, now back to our dinner in Therese's home. Returning to the kitchen with the celery, I help chop veggies for the Greek salad. Ed cooks fish for the main course served at a table beautifully set by Therese with her lovely linens, cutlery, and a big bouquet of flowers at one end. Everything is delicious and the conversation flows easily and with much laughter.

Our time in Bruges is almost over. How could it have gone by so fast? Harriet has reassured me that I can come and stay with her again next year and she suggests June. I would like that as Bruges is my most favorite place to be.

I do have other favorite places in the world and, after Bruges, one is Molokai, an island in Hawaii. Not many tourists go there so it is not as busy as the other islands. I like that about it. Our first time in Molokai in 1987, I read about a leper colony that was established there in 1866 in Kalaupapa, a very remote place where the only access was by sea, through heavy surf. The peninsula juts seaward from a base of cliffs over a thousand feet high. People with leprosy were sent there for permanent exile and lived in very primitive, unsanitary conditions.

Father Damien, a Belgian priest came to the leper colony in 1873 and conditions gradually improved under his care. I couldn't believe what I have read. He could have come from any country but it was Belgium and, even better, he was from the Flemish area. He died on Kalaupapa in 1889 after developing leprosy.

Ed and I are sitting on our lanai on Molokai and I say, "We could go to Kalaupapa and see where the leper colony is but we would have to go by mule!"

"What?"

"In 1886, a supply route was built to the settlement below. Now, you can ride a mule down the 1600-foot-high cliff on a trail with twenty-six switchbacks to the leper colony below."

"Do you want to do that?"

"It sounds rather scary but I would like to do it. I can't imagine riding a mule, can you?"

"I think it would be interesting to see you riding on a mule! Let's go for it," says Ed.

We arrange the mule ride for the next day. There are twelve people in our group.

The guide advises, "Hold on to the reins, but you don't need to direct the mule. They know the trail very well."

My mule is named Roman and I climb up onto his back. They place the mules in a certain order and Ed, much nearer to the front, starts off before me. Roman starts to move to the top of the cliff and then steps down and goes along the side. I expect Roman to follow in the footsteps of the mule in front of him so I bend slightly preparing for the drop to the right, but no, he steps to the left. And so it continues as Roman decides where he is going! Down, down we go, continually making switchbacks. I tend to look down more at the path instead of the surrounding cliff-side views.

I'm relieved when, at the bottom, I am helped down from the mule. It feels good to stand on my own two feet. We tour the settlement and hear a talk about Father Damien. I say to Ed,

"I just can't believe what Father Damien did to improve the conditions for the people with leprosy. And to think, he came from Belgium, and the Flemish part near Bruges!"

I am reminded of another story about a priest. In the summer of 1952, I took a job in the information bureau for the Alberta Motor Association in Jasper National Park. I learned about a priest, Father Pierre Jean de Smet who was from Europe and came to America in the 1880s. In the early spring of 1846, he was in the Jasper area and noticed how strong the current was in the confluence of two rivers. In his journal he called this "maligne," a French word for wicked or treacherous. The name "Maligne" was eventually used not only for the river, but also for the lake, the canyon, and the mountain. In 1952, when I was there, there was no public road to Maligne Lake or canyon, but I was able to travel there with a small group over back roads. I loved it!

So many, many years later, after going to Bruges I learned that Father Pierre Jean de Smet was from the town of Dendermonde in the Flemish part of Belgium. He was of Flemish peasant stock, well loved by everyone for his enthusiasm and good spirits. I can't even imagine what it would have been like to travel in America at that time.

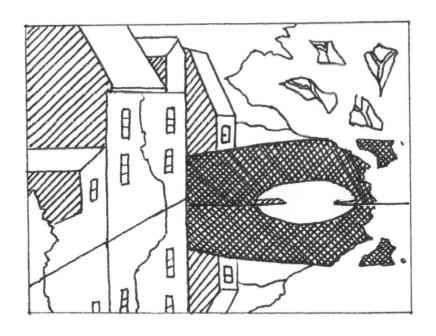

Chapter 14

Where Did It All Start?

I 'm having an affair, an affair with the medieval city of Bruges. It has gone on for years. I'm drawn to this place again and again and the excitement is still there. Why am I always being drawn back? It touches me deep in my soul. It gives me a feeling of peace. I'm able to truly live in the moment. Why? How? There are always new discoveries to be made about my love. My city welcomes me, holds me, nourishes me, shows me beauty, and gives me joy and laughter that comes spontaneously. It shows me reflections in the canals, reflections so perfect that the line between reflection and reality hardly matters. I wonder… is this all a dream? What is real?

Who am I? Who *was* I? These questions keep floating in and out of my consciousness. I keep looking for logical answers for what is happening to me in Bruges, but they don't come.

Will it help to write it all down? Will it become clear to me? What is this love affair that I have with a medieval city? Why do tears fall when I leave? That is what happens in a love affair, as one wants to be with their beloved.

Can I make sense of it? I've put off writing about it until I can make sense of it. But that may never happen. I must write about it. Maybe writing it all down will make sense of it! All I know is that I keep being drawn back to Bruges again and again, and when I'm there, certain places silently draw me to them. I follow and go but I do not understand.

I believe something is calling me back from hundreds and hundreds of years ago. I must have lived there in medieval times. Who was I? Where did I live? Why does the Beguinage call so strongly to me? Was I a Beguine? I feel very peaceful when I walk the paths in front of the Beguinage. Why am I called back at this time in my life?

I stand at the top of the stairs. I look down, down, down. The stairs seem to twist and turn. I tentatively start down. I hear a voice in my head saying, "Go deeper." I continue down then pause, and once again the words, "Go deeper." How can I go any deeper? It is starting to get dark but I can still see cobwebs clinging to the walls. I continue on but when I stop, I do not hear the words, "Go deeper."

I feel a desire to go back up and as I begin to turn a voice says, "Stay." I turn back and see a door in front of me. I stare at it and then knock quietly. The door swings open and I see a large room with windows all along the far wall. There are large couches and chairs and small tables and chairs just the right size for small children. Slowly I gaze all around but I can see no one. Through the windows I see there are green leaves everywhere and huge ancient trees with gnarled branches and twisted shapes. None of them is straight and tall.

I hear music, the sound of a harp. It seems to waft in and float through the air, but I can't see a harp nor determine just where the sound is coming from. I sit awhile on a green velvet couch but soon I'm drawn to look out the window again and gaze at the trees. Suddenly, I'm on a cobblestoned street and I'm wearing a long black gown and my hair is covered. I see another woman dressed as I am and she comes to me and says,

"Come inside. Sister Francis has words for us. Why are you hesitating? Come."

I see others dressed as we are. They are seated on hard, straight-backed chairs. I quietly sit down beside the woman who has brought me. I don't know where I am but I somehow feel that I belong here!

A tall woman, dressed as the others, comes in. Everyone stands and it is very quiet. The woman signals for us to sit down. She smiles and says,

"I have good news. Countess Margaret of Constantinople is going to help us. She will establish an area here in Brugge for us. We Beguines will be able to live here on our own and go out from here to care for the sick and give help to others."

I glance around and everyone looks relieved and pleased. Church bells begin to ring. Suddenly, I'm back sitting on the green velvet couch. I look down at my clothing but it is not black. I shake my head and my hair moves freely. It can't have been a dream. I was somewhere else. I know I was and I liked being there.

Again I look out the windows and see the tree branches. I remember walking to the window and looking out and then, I am somewhere else. How could that be? I stand up and begin to slowly walk to the window. A wind is blowing, the branches are moving and the leaves are fluttering. Suddenly I am on my mauve and pink shaggy horse and we're galloping through a starlit sky. My hair is blowing behind me. I feel so free as we continue to gallop through the night. And then just as suddenly, I'm back sitting on the green velvet couch. Everything is so still and quiet. Where is the wind in my face and the stars lighting up the dark sky and my hair blowing in the wind and my freedom? Where is it?

I get up from the couch and go to the door. It is still open and I leave. I do not hear voices telling me what to do so I turn and start to climb the winding stairs. The cobwebs get fewer and fewer and still no voices are telling me what to do. Do I keep climbing, or turn back, or stay still?

I come to the last few steps and quicken my pace and reach the top, open the door and I'm back in my home. I walk slowly and thoughtfully to my kitchen and make a pot of tea, which I then take to my couch with its muted green and pink floral pattern. From there I can look out the window at my trees and garden, at birds busily flitting about, at my flowers. I see a large

> *pink peony just opening up. What beauty! As the*
> *days pass, the peony will continue to change and*
> *slowly evolve to show its true beauty.*

Why am I drawn to Bruges? It has given me much joy and new friends, new experiences and a place that makes me feel as if I truly live there! I keep going back and back. I need to write about it and follow all the connections back and back through years and years. The word "back" keeps surfacing in my thoughts. It clarifies that it is not forward that I have to go, but back and back.

Do I need this peacefulness in my life at this time? My first time in Bruges was linked to a trip to Norway to meet with Debbie, my oldest daughter. It seems as if Bruges was a refuge set up for me, to help me with what I had to face that I knew nothing of at the time, something that needed to be put in place and later it helped me in my grief.

Belgium is also interesting to me as it has a French speaking region and a Flemish speaking region. I was once in Brussels, the French part, but I was not drawn back there. It was only when I visited Flemish Bruges that something captured me. Something that will not let go!

Upon reflection, throughout my life I can trace things that were, though I didn't realize it then, drawing me to Bruges. In my early teen years, I remember looking through some old books of my mother's to find one of interest to me, one that I felt drawn to. Mom looks at the one I have chosen and says,

"I'm sure that you'll like it. I must have read it when I was about fourteen."

The book is titled "Marieken De Bruin" and subtitled, "Somewhere in Belgium," and the author is Martha Trent. I take the book into the living room, curl up in a chair and start to read. The story is set in the First World War and the Germans have invaded a small Flemish village. Marieken is the fourteen-year-old daughter of the innkeeper who has been killed. His one son is away in the Belgian Army and so Marieken and her sick mother are running the inn.

"This is really good. I don't want to stop reading," I say to Mom as I reluctantly set the table for dinner.

The Second World War is currently happening so I'm aware of war and the Germans. I can relate to Marieken and her feelings about the Germans who stay at the Inn. Marieken is brave and stands up to them at times. She can also speak German, so that helps. As I continue to read, I'm immersed in the world of Marieken, with her attempts to deal with the German occupation and with her work with the Resistance. I read the book every chance I get and finish it very quickly.

After World War Two is over, my Uncle Bert returns home. He was stationed in Brussels, Belgium for part of the war. I'm intrigued that he was actually in Belgium because of my experience reading a book set in Belgium in the First World War. When I go next door to visit my grandma, she points to a new object on her mantel and says,

"Look at what Bert brought back from Brussels."

I walk closer and see a small bronze statue of a little boy urinating. I am slightly shocked! Grandma says, "It is a copy of a famous statue in Brussels called the *Mannekin Pis.* It was done in the 1600s." How strange. Does Grandma really like it? Will she leave it on her mantel?

One day, years later when I'm married and the very busy mother of three children, I sit down to have a quick look at a magazine before Barbara wakes up from her nap. I stop at an article on Winston Churchill's paintings. Some of them are shown and I feel an immediate attraction to one. It shows tall trees all bending in the same direction and a large grassed courtyard encircled by whitewashed, red-roofed houses. On a path through the trees, there are several nuns dressed in habits of long black tunics and white headpieces walking meditatively on the paths. I stare at the picture. It looks so peaceful. I imagine how it would feel to be walking there.

I hear Barbara and go to pick her up.

"Did you have a nice nap?"

I nuzzle her warm neck and bring her to the living room. I sit her down on the rug and bring a few toys for her and I once more look at the magazine picture. It covers a full page and I decide to cut it out and pin it up on our bedroom wall. Afterwards I stand back and then lower it just a bit. I get a warm feeling whenever I look at it. I hope that Ed likes the picture! And he does!

Many years later after our first two trips to Bruges and having been so surprised and moved by seeing the actual setting of Churchill's painting, I decide to find out more information about it. I don't know what happened to the picture on our bedroom wall. Did it wrinkle? Was it thrown away when we moved to another house? What was it called? This requires research so I head to the library and look up collections of Churchill's paintings. At a table I begin looking through one book and become very excited when I find it, a beautiful oil painting. Yes, it is what I've seen, the tall trees all leaning in one direction, the large grassy courtyard encircled by the whitewashed, red-roofed Beguine houses. Something that I hadn't remembered about his painting was that the three nuns walking on the path are looking down at an open book in their hands. Beyond the houses to the left, I can see the tall spire of the Church of Our Lady. It is beautiful. I look to see what gallery this painting is in. I discover that it was painted in 1946 and has been in a private collection since 1962. How sad, as I would have liked to be able to see it. I look for the title of the painting and it is, "Le Beguinage, Bruges." I must have once seen the title but the name Bruges would have meant nothing to me. I'd always thought that the title was "Somewhere in Belgium" but now I realize that those words were a subtitle in the Marieken book that I read in my teens.

I take the Churchill book home to show Ed.

"I'll never get to see the original painting but if it was in a museum in England, then I might."

135

"He does capture it very well."

"Yes, there is definitely that feeling of peacefulness. It is done in oil and I would have thought that watercolor could capture it better. But what do I know about painting! I'm going to get a copy of this. It'll just be in black and white but it is part of Bruges and I want to have it."

Years later in Bruges, after I have met Harriet, I learn even more about the painting. I'm sitting in my favorite spot in her kitchen by the window overlooking the canal. Harriet's friend Jeanine is visiting with her. Jeanine was born in Bruges where she lived for many years before she married and moved to Paris. She asks me,

"Margaret, where have you been walking today?"

"I've just been at the Beguinage walking around the paths. It's incredible that I saw Churchill's painting of the Beguinage in a magazine so many years ago and now I'm enjoying seeing what he painted."

Jeanine looks at me and says, "I was here in 1946 and saw Churchill painting that picture! He was sitting on a chair on the lawn and had an easel set up. There were some guards near him."

"And you were actually there? How special! I would have loved to have seen that!"

On one of my Bruges trips, I attend a concert in the Church of Our Lady. The music is all Bach with some organ, some choral, some solos, and also instrumental works. As the choir begins to sing, I feel a warmth spreading through my chest and I am on the verge of tears. There is definitely something in the church that speaks to me. I vividly remember the first time I was there and I had that incredible moment as a deep feeling passed through me. It is so difficult to express in words. It happens so quickly and so totally unexpectedly. If I try to recapture it, I cannot. In other places in Bruges I've had this intensely moving experience when I seem to become filled with light, my chest feeling as if it could break with the depth of feeling—so overwhelming, and yet I am always left with a marvellous feeling of peace.

Chapter 15

Unexpected Happenings

August 25, 1998, I arrive at Harriet's. I will stay in her garret for three weeks before Ed arrives and then together we will stay at Therese's for ten days. After my arrival, Harriet tells me some disturbing news. Odette's husband Georges isn't well and it is quite serious. I feel very sad about this and decide to visit them soon.

My walk in the sunshine helps with my jet lag but I can't bear to go past Lislie's house as she has only just died in June. Being here in Bruges and not seeing Lislie just doesn't seem right. The next day, I go to see Odette and Georges. I am surprised to see how wonderful Georges looks. He has lost weight and his face just seems to glow. When he hugs me, I get tears. He says that he hopes to get in a sightseeing trip once Ed arrives.

Odette invites me for lunch tomorrow. She is taking it well. Her strength is there. Ed will be devastated by the news. We so enjoy Georges.

Oh, how can this be? Lislie's death in June and now Georges is very ill. I learn that he has pancreatic cancer and has decided not to take chemotherapy.

A few days later, I go for a long walk and just let myself go to where I am drawn, even past Lislie's house where I look in the window at the emptiness. So many memories of her fill my thoughts as I walk around the Beguinage. That afternoon, I take tea with Therese and enjoy a good visit. In the evening, Harriet, Odette and I have been invited to a remembrance tribute to Lislie, a get-together of her friends followed by an organ concert in her memory. Odette won't be going but Harriet and I will attend.

I am immersed in the company of these good women, my Bruges friends, enjoying tea with Therese in her sunny medieval garden, then an evening with Harriet in a restaurant to meet with Lislie's friends. I know some of them and listen to their conversation while I sip my red wine and eat a delicious lasagne. Flemish is mostly spoken but Harriet translates for me, some there and then more afterwards. It all helps to put some closure on Lislie's death.

I've been here a week now and feel the need to settle into some writing. Harriet's friend Betty has lent me her typewriter to use while I'm here. Actually, it can operate a bit like a computer. It can insert and make changes and save them and print them out. I don't want to bother with all of that so she shows me how to use it as a regular typewriter. As we seem to be having a lot of rainstorms, it is a good time to stay in and write!

I love how content and peaceful I feel here. I used to think that being in the Beguinage gave me this but not so. It is definitely to do with Bruges itself, the essence of Bruges. Now I need to bask in this essence and restore my soul.

I've put in a good effort before the phone rings. It's late in the afternoon and Odette is calling to ask me if I could come for a visit. When I arrive, Georges is sleeping but, after our own excellent visit, we go again to see Georges. He is in Odette's painting room, on her couch, peacefully gazing out the window. Georges's face looks good but his body is definitely weaker. We chat for a bit and then we all go downstairs where Odette feeds us a light supper of soup and veggies and tapioca pudding.

Back in my garret, I am writing. Bells are ringing again, always when I'm writing and there is the constant cooing of doves. I can't believe how peaceful I feel!

September 6

Time is passing. Georges is becoming weaker. I do some writing today and as it begins to flow, I feel enthused about it. It feels so different writing today. Maybe my "off" day yesterday was my turning point. It has taken me close to two weeks to unwind. Harriet has asked me to a concert tonight in the Church of Our Lady. It is a lovely evening, an all-Bach concert featuring vocal music, some strings, and organ music, and followed up with a wine and cheese reception.

A few days later, when I am out for a walk, a car stops near me and the driver asks me for directions. This is the fourth time that I've been asked for directions on this trip and I'm always happy to be helpful. I walk for a while, do some shopping, and arrive back just as rain begins to fall. It is already two, time for a quick lunch. Then I begin to write for an hour or more and it feels so good.

I'm in a wonderful self-learning process, and not living to a definite time schedule is certainly different. I like the way I can suddenly decide to do something and then do it! Surprise myself. This is the first time that I have spent three weeks on my own before Ed's arrival. Here at Harriet's, I have my own space and my own schedule.

September 11

I just learned that Georges died yesterday and the funeral will be on the sixteenth. Ed arrives on the fifteenth so he'll be able to attend the funeral.

Today, September 12, there is a slashing rain, hitting against the windows and the roof. I settle down at the typewriter and I seem to move back into a time many centuries ago.

Another Life

I live my life by the sound of church bells. What a comforting sound it is to me. Oh, now I hear the sound of horse's hooves on the cobblestones. Pierre must be on his way. What news will he bring? Hopefully Father's cough is better. Home seems so far away but now that I'm here, this is my home.

How can I be so peaceful and contented when there is so much trouble elsewhere? I'm happy that I'm not a young mother with many children to feed and look after. As long as I can remember, I have never wanted that. My friends did and they could hardly wait for it. Thank goodness for Mother Sophia as she could always see that there was another life for me. But Father was strong in his belief that Pierre was to become a priest and I was to remain at home and help Mother with the younger children and in time, I would be married to an older capable man.

I owe my escape to Pierre, my twin brother who spoke up for me and said that I should be the one to go to the Church and become a nun, as he had no desire to live the life of a priest. It took some time but eventually Pierre did convince Father to let me be the one to go. And I have never regretted doing that.

I sit in my room and think back, way back to when I first came here. I had no doubts then that this was the life that I wanted. Oh yes, I did have some timidity and also knew that I was expected to be this way at the beginning. I seemed to move into this life as if I had known it all before, as if I had an inner guide. Would Pierre have liked the priesthood? I think not as I watch him with his five children. He is a happy man and his wife, Mary, is a happy woman, one born to be a mother. Pierre is fortunate, indeed.

I hear the sound of the front doorbell. Sister Anne will open it for Pierre and show him into the small sitting room. I'll go down before she has to come and get me. I meet Sister Anne at the bottom of the front stairs. As she starts to speak, I say, "I know. Pierre is here. Thank you, Sister."

In the sitting room, Pierre is standing looking out the window and he turns as he hears the rustle of my approach. His cheeks are rosy, his eyes still have their twinkle and his ruddy-coloured hair has a few white streaks. Pierre takes my shoulders and gives me a kiss on each cheek. "Good to see you, Pierre. How is Father?"

"Much improved and now that the weather is starting to warm up, his cough may totally leave."

"How is Mother?"

"Busy with the grandchildren. She has been helping Bridget out with her new baby. The baby seems quite sickly and cries a lot."

"How difficult for Bridget! She always seems so busy with her other three children."

"We're hoping to have everyone together to celebrate Mother's birthday and they all want you to come. Will you be able to?"

"Oh, I think so. Are you having it on her actual birth date?"

"Yes, I think so. I'll write you after I talk to our sisters and Matthew."

"Thank you for coming, Pierre. I knew it was your horse that I heard. What rosy cheeks you have from the ride."

"Good-bye Amelia,"

"Good-bye. Give my love to Mary and the children."

A few days later, Pierre's note arrives. What lovely penmanship he has, much better than mine. He will come to get me on the seventeenth and says that his children are excited about seeing me. He adds that Mother is becoming very frail and now walks with a cane. How nice it will be to see them all.

Many Years Later

I look out on a snowy landscape. How unfamiliar to me. In all the years that I've been here there has only been a snowfall like this twice before. I settle back to my letter reading. The papers are old and wrinkled, just like me, ancient, letters from my earliest days here with the sisters. Nearly all my letters are from family. I reread their news of activities, celebrations and the different things that have happened to them. I've never wished to leave here. I made my decision and it was the right one. I have Pierre and Father to thank for that.

Father has been dead for a long time and Mother before him. I fold the letters and replace them in my wooden box, which I put away on my shelf with my few possessions. But what would I have wanted that I don't have? I can think of nothing. The church bells are ringing, time to go and pray.

September 15

I'm up early to a light grey sky, but no rain. Ed will be on the plane, sleeping, I hope, but around 10 o'clock, I get a phone call from him and he is still in Calgary! His plane blew an engine on take-off and it is now 2:30 in the early morning and he is finally at a hotel. He doesn't know when he'll fly out! Air Canada is just coming off a strike so he can't transfer to them. Everyone is scrambling to get to Europe. It is strange as I wrote about Ed sleeping on the plane, I had a twinge of a doubt but I dismissed it. Thank God that he is safe, but what a shock.

Later I go for a walk. The sun feels so good. It would have been a nice day for Ed to arrive. Oh Ed, where are you? On a plane, on a train, on a bus, or just waiting somewhere?

Just before ten, I go to the funeral in the Church of Our Lady, my first funeral in Bruges. It lasts about one-and-a-half hours during which time my tears flow. Odette asks me if I would like to have a meal with them. I accept and we go to the graveyard and then to a hotel for a meal. It feels so nice to be included with family and a few close friends. I wish Ed could have been here to experience this.

I return to Harriet's just after four hoping that Ed will have arrived but there is no word from him. What has happened? When will he get here? I feel totally fatigued from this very emotional day. Harriet has just gone out but I feel the need to be here in case Ed phones or arrives. I hate the waiting, the not knowing, but I feel that he may be here within the hour. I will have to wait and see! At five ten, Ed arrives. I was right!

We take his luggage to Therese's and then we go out for dinner and talk and talk.

There are flowers and fruit in our room and, of course, the lovely big bed. Ed is only here for nine days. We go off for a day with Odette to Oostende, a sunny day, great for walking along the beach. Another day, Ed is off to the fish market, which he so enjoys, and he has bought fish and cooked it for Therese and Harriet and me. Delicious!

When Ed and I talk about next year's trip, I ask,

"I wonder if I should come first again next year?"

"Oh, yes, I think that it is so good for you."

A few more days go by and I believe that I'm starting to withdraw from Bruges. My body probably knows that I have to start the process. Next week at this time I'll be back home!

Exploring with
Odette - 2003

I walk down a narrow cobblestone street on my way to visit Odette. On my left in the yellow sidewall of an art gallery, there is an opening, much like a large open window, that allows one to gaze into the garden. I slow down to look inside. On a bench sits a figure, a beautiful woman, a statue, but she looks so real. She sits with her hands folded in her lap and her feet crossed at the ankles. She is not in the middle of the bench but closer to one end. Is she waiting for someone to join her? Hanging behind her on the yellow wall is a birdcage with a top like a church dome, and several other little white birdhouses with slanted roofs. There are some small round trees and lovely pink flowers highlighted by the yellow wall. It all looks so special and inviting.

I walk on, turn left and glance into the front window of the gallery. A clay sculpture of a nude woman captures my attention. Her legs are bent and her head is resting on her arm. It reminds me of the child's pose in yoga, a pose that I like to do. The sculpture is about nine inches in length. I love it. There is no price but there is a name underneath beginning with an "N." Is it the name of a goddess or a mythical figure? I've never seen the name. I stand looking at it a little longer and then continue down the street to Odette's.

When I arrive, she is already backing her car out of the garage. We're going to Zevenkerken. We like to go walking in the forest and afterwards sit outside on the huge lawn, dotted with apple trees, and have tea or coffee and sweets at an outdoor table.

As we drive along, I say,

"I saw a lovely sculpture in the window of the gallery at the end of your street. I really liked it. Some name was written on a card in front of it. I didn't know the word but it started with the letter "N".

"I don't know what it would be but we can have a look when we get back. I know the owner, Paul. He's very nice. If his bicycle is parked outside, he'll still be there."

Odette drives over a bridge and we leave Bruges behind as we head onto a highway.

She says,

"I've biked out here a few times this past summer. Would you like to try it? I still have Georges' bike and you could use it or mine."

"You biked all the way to Zevenkerken? How far is it?"

"Just a nice trip, only about twelve miles."

"Odette, that is far, twenty-four miles round trip! As for bicycling, I haven't been on a bike since I was seventeen! If I lived here, I probably would bike but in Canada, it is all cars and cars."

We drive through lush countryside and picturesque small towns. Always once you've gone through a town, a sign in Flemish says --You are now leaving _____-- and the name of the town is written in large letters. I recall how years before when Ed and I were driving in Belgium and trying to find out where we were, we would see the large name of the town and think that we were just going to enter it! After a while we figured it out.

There is always something to see: trees, church steeples, farmhouses, and cows. Not at all like where I grew up with prairie all around, what seemed to be an endless landscape without any houses or farms, and certainly not any steeples.

Eventually Odette drives through a large open gate and down a road lined with beautiful tall trees on each side. All of a sudden, it feels protective and serene. Odette drives in further and parks in a space between two trees.

"Are we going to walk first?"

"Yes, let's do that and then we can have something to eat after."

"Sounds great, I'll just grab my water bottle," I say.

A short way along, we enter an opening in the trees to a well-worn path with trees stretching as far as we can see on either side.

"I love walking here. There seems to be such peacefulness. How ancient is this?"

"It was founded as an abbey in the 1100s and was destroyed at one time, then later rebuilt."

"So these paths have been walked on by monks," I say.

"Yes, and they still are though this is more of a public area. But there are other paths."

We continue to walk in silence. How happy I am to be with a person who also treasures this meditative quiet.

"Odette, I would like to take a picture of you with the trees behind."

"No, let me take one of you," and she holds out her hand for my camera. I give it to her and ask,

"Where do you want me to stand?"

"Nowhere, just start walking."

I slowly start to walk ahead of her. I continue and then turn to ask her if she wants me to stop and I hear the camera click.

"I didn't know that you were going to take it."

"I like to take pictures before people realize it. Much more natural that way."

"Ah… that must be the artist in you coming out."

We continue walking. I spot a pretty white flower and bend down and cup it with my hands. How beautiful. And just then, I hear the click of the camera!

"Odette, did you just take another picture?"

"It'll be perfect, you and the flower!"

On we go letting the silence enfold us. I see a small path veering off from our larger one.

"How about that path? It looks interesting."

"We're really not supposed to go off this path but let's explore it."

"Are you sure it'll be alright?" I ask as we start down the narrow, dark path. When we arrive at a large open area, I immediately walk to an enormous tree and stand under it.

"What a beautiful tree! Look at the size of the trunk. What kind is it?"

"It is an oak."

Odette looks around and points in the direction we need to go.

"I'm glad you know the way because I certainly don't."

Eventually we come to the large outdoor eating area. With some delicious looking apricot tarts, coffee for Odette and tea for me, we choose a table outside under trees in the far corner. Here we sit and eat, drink, talk and just relax.

"I sometimes come here on my own to sit and read or do some sketches."

"How peaceful, especially in this corner. Odette, remember a few years ago when I was fussing about something, you looked at me and said, "Remember, life is easy."

"I remember that. We were on the little bridge by the Beguinage."

We sit quietly enjoying the warm sunlight filtering through the trees. I take out my camera.

"I want to take a picture of you sitting right here under the apple tree."

I walk across the lawn, turn, start to focus and just then, Odette turns her head slightly. I snap the picture.

"That should be a nice one. I wanted one of you in this setting. Back home, I'll look at it and remember our lovely time here. Oh, listen to the church bells."

"Yes, in five minutes, the monks will begin their chanting. We can go and listen, if you want."

"I would like to but I just don't feel like rushing there right now. Could we do it the next time we come here?"

"Yes, that will work out better. Some days they do longer chants but today, it is just a short one."

"Sounds like you go often."

"If I'm here and I feel like it, I go. I love hearing and watching them chanting."

Odette drives out the gate, leaving behind the serenity as we wait for a break in traffic to enter the highway. Closer to Bruges there is more traffic. We line up to cross one of the bridges that will take us into the city. I sigh and feel happy to be back in Bruges again. As we drive down Odette's street, she says,

"Paul's bicycle is there. I'll go with you to the gallery after I put the car in the garage."

Looking in the window, I point out the figure to Odette and she says,

"It is lovely. You will enjoy having this."

"What does that word say?"

"It is the Flemish word for "Nude.""

"Oh, is that it? How perfect, as that is what it is. I do want to know the price."

"Come on, let's go in and I'll introduce you."

Odette rings the bell and a tall man with bushy red hair and a full face greets us. Odette says,

"This is my friend Margaret and she is interested in something in your window."

Paul shakes my hand. "Show me." I point out the figure and he picks it up and hands it to me. I hold it and look at it more closely. It is beautiful. I learn that it is by a local artist.

"How much is it?" I ask.

Paul quotes a price in Euros and I quickly attempt to think what that will be in Canadian money. I look at Paul and say,

"Yes, I would like to buy it. Could you put it away for me until tomorrow? I'll come by and pay you then. I just don't have that amount with me right now."

"That is just fine. I'll put it aside for you."

"I saw your bike and told Margaret that you would still be here."

"You just caught me. I was just going to close."

"Thanks. I'll see you tomorrow."

We shake hands at the door and leave.

I comment to Odette, "He seemed very nice."

"Oh, he is a very nice fellow. He has another gallery in a more central part of town and his wife is at that one. But Paul is usually here where he does his own artwork and also where he can decide on the hours that the gallery is open."

"Thanks for being with me. I can't wait to come back and get my nude!"

"I'm going to Oostende tomorrow but you could come to my place on Thursday around noon and we can have some lunch and then go somewhere, maybe to Sluis, if you want."

We hug and I go down to the corner and turn and wave to Odette. It is something that we have done for ages. I reach the corner and glance back and she is always there to give me a quick wave. It makes me think of my childhood years when Dad would drive us to the farm to visit our grandparents and as we drove away, we would look through the back window and see them standing and waving until we could no longer see them.

Chapter 17

An Aha Moment

The next afternoon I return to the gallery. When I look in the front window, I see the empty space where my figure was. I ring the bell and Paul opens the door. I am greeted with soft classical music. I glance around as he goes to get my figure and through an open door, I see there is a workroom with paintings on a table. From the main gallery there is a view out a back window to a bit of the garden. I move closer to a table where Paul is wrapping my figure.

He says, "You have lived here before."

"Yes, I've been coming here for years."

"You have lived at least four lifetimes here, starting probably in the 1200s and up till the 1800s."

I feel tears beginning to form as I say, "I first visited here many years ago and always there is something that draws me back again and again."

"You have completed your karma here. You now come back when you need nourishment. It revives you."

"How wonderful to have someone understand how I feel!" I am overwhelmed. Tears are now falling down my face. I feel in my jacket pocket but there is no tissue, and none in my purse. I'm blubbering. I look up at Paul with my tear-stained face and ask, "Do you have a tissue?"

He isn't at all perturbed and goes into another room and brings back a paper towel. I wipe my face and nose and clear my throat. The music continues to play. It is so peaceful here. My parcel is wrapped but Paul continues to talk. I'm amazed at what he tells me and how it just flows out of him. I finally pay him for the figure but I don't want to leave. Paul says, "Please keep what I have said to yourself." And of course I will! I am so touched, so shocked that finally I have found someone who understands what I experience in Bruges. This is a very private moment.

"Have you always lived in Bruges?" I inquire.

"I was born here but later, I went away to India for some years. But I was drawn back. There is some powerful energy here and very ancient energy, a great place to be."

I thank him and we hug and then I walk slowly back to Harriet's. I can hardly believe what has happened. I'm stunned by it and yet I feel so calm and peaceful. It was so intriguing to talk with him and so validating to have someone understand how I feel here. I did live here before. I really, really did! How very special!

At Harriet's I go up the thirty-five steps to my garret. I can hear the rain begin to fall. I open my parcel. It was this figure that drew me into that gallery. I have gone past it for a number of years but have never felt drawn to go in. I place the sculpture on the small wicker coffee table. I'll be able to look at it as I do my morning journal writing. What will Ed think of it when he comes in ten days? My heart feels so full. I love it. I'm glad that I bought it.

What Paul told me seemed to flow out of him so effortlessly. I believe in reincarnation. Did I once live in this house of Harriet's? Why have I felt so at home here since the first day that I walked into her house? Why do I always want to sit in the same kitchen chair looking out the window in one direction? Why am I so happy in Bruges? Why is it easier for me to live in the moment here? Paul's revelation certainly helps to answer some of these questions.

On Ed's arrival day, I hear the doorbell and hurry down the thirty-five steps. Harriet has answered and she and Ed are already sharing a hug. Then it is my turn. Ed and I have a long hug. It is great to see him again. We all head to Harriet's kitchen for tea and goodies.

We talk about Ed's flight and I ask him,

"How did the two train connections go?"

He laughs and says, "I only had to make the one connection."

"No! How come? I had to make two, rushing down the concrete steps and then up to the other platform with so little time to do it. I can't believe that you didn't have to do that!"

"Well, I guess whatever caused the change has now been corrected."

"I had thought that it was going to be in effect for months."

I look at Ed and think how good he looks even with the jet lag. He has been flying all night and with the eight-hour time change, I know what he must be feeling. We talk some more with Harriet and then head upstairs to my garret abode. The first thing Ed notices is my sculpture.

"I bought it at the gallery near Odette's. I just loved it and decided that I had to have it."

Ed says, "It's beautiful. I really like it."

I turn it around slightly so that he sees her head more than her derriere! We laugh and Ed stands up and we hug.

"I really missed you."

I look at him and say, "Yes, I missed you, too."

Chapter 18

And Time Moves On…

At times, I wonder if this seems to be like a travelogue, but I'm really only attempting to capture and relate the wonders of Bruges and how it is that I keep being drawn back again and again.

In late August of 2007, I'm once again staying in Harriet's garret and will be on my own for two weeks before Ed will arrive. It is a lovely day and I have two windows open allowing in a refreshing breeze and the sound of the canal boats going past. Oh, the sun just came out and it is definitely time for a walk to the Beguinage.

As I walk the paths across the Beguinage lawns, I can hear harp music. Where is it coming from? I follow the sound and as I exit the Beguinage, I see a man sitting near the Minnewater Lake playing a very large harp. It is absolutely beautiful music and in such a perfect setting near an ancient tree with the lake beyond. Many people are standing around listening and enjoying his music. I listen for a while and then go walking further along the lake, eventually returning to the harp player. He has stopped playing and I talk with him about the CD of his music, which he has on display. The recording, *Ebb Tide,* with a cover showing ocean, rocks, and beach, is all his original music. This music really speaks to me as I love the ocean, the sound of the waves and the immensity of it all. Harpist Luc Vanlaere is happy to sell me a CD tomorrow, as I have no money with me today.

A number of years later, it has now become a part of my "Bruges time" to attend one of Luc's concerts. These are now performed indoors at Old St. John.

An interesting day to walk in Bruges is Friday, the day of weddings. As I walk around, I see brides and grooms posing before the Lake of Love, or on a stone bridge, or on a stone wall with the bride scampering on top of the wall, laughing and hanging on to her groom and then lifting her dress to display the garter on her leg. The photographer continues to pose them for more and more pictures. Sometimes the bride and groom and the wedding party go for a boat ride on the canals. Swans also float on the canal. Sometimes a baby swan goes for a ride nestled comfortably on the back of the mother swan as she glides majestically down the canal.

Back home, I'm ready to look at my writing, ready to write more. I think of Bruges and the canals and the trees, many ancient ones. I so love the trees. But what is beyond the trees? Will I never get there? Can I really make my way through the trees to the other side? What will be there? Another barrier, or a safe place? There is no way that I can know ahead of time. I just have to make my way through the trees. Will I have to go around obstacles? Will I have to backtrack? Will I have to climb up high in a tree and attempt to see a path? Will the tree's branches help me to move forward or will they hinder me? Will I ask for help if I need it or will I attempt to do it all on my own? Will the sunlight shine through at times or will it be eternally dark? Will I take time to look for flowers, to watch and listen to birds, to curl up and nap beneath a tree? I must continue my journey. The leaves are just beginning to fall from the trees. Can I cope with winter? Do I need to pause in my journey and go even deeper? I must allow myself the pauses. They are part of the journey.

A fuzzy caterpillar just came to see me. It walked across my desk and looked me in the eye and said:

"Do you realize that this is not what I'll always be? I will undergo change and grow wings, beautifully coloured wings, and I will fly! No more crawling along the ground. I'll be able to soar and go much further than I could while crawling. As for you, your writing will change, too. You will learn to soar, to flow, to move beyond. Believe me, I know."

Chapter 19

I'll Be Back

I 've written a lot about Bruges and now I feel the need to talk with Paul, about what he has told me about living in Bruges many centuries ago. I finally contact him close to my departure day from Bruges. I ask him if I can put what he has told me about my past lives into my book about my love affair with Bruges. He replies: "Of course! You need to write that book. Write it and next year when you come back, you can just play!"

The church bells begin to ring and ring and I know that I am back in Bruges. How could I have been away for so long? I breathe deeply and feel the sound of the bells entering my soul. I hurry outside and walk and walk the cobblestone streets to my favorite bridge over the canal. I stand and gaze at the reflections of trees and buildings and sky and listen as the bells continue to ring. I'm back. I'm back. I feel such calmness in my being. I am radiant, like a bride moving quickly out of the church and being showered with confetti.

I love it. I love it. My love affair with Bruges continues. I call out, "I'm here. I'm back and I'm staying for a long time." The church bells continue to peal and the wind causes a ripple in the reflections. I cross the bridge and move toward the sound of the bells.

Bells

Bells forever ringing
Through day and evening.
Tones of hope, tones of joy
Peal upon peal.
Thus from ancient times
Many have heard the call.
Be uplifted, live with joy.

Ding dong, ding dong, ding dong.
Bells have tolled before you
And bells will toll after you.
On, on, and on forever thus.

Nearly always in Bruges, the sound of bells, an ancient sound calling community. The bells echo within me. The cobblestone streets beckoning my footsteps, "Come this way, Margaret" and later, "Sit on this bench by the water, the lake." I do, and the stillness enters my soul. The inner voice becomes clearer. My body becomes flooded with peacefulness and joy and I feel the connection to myself, to spirit, and to all humanity.

Acknowledgements

Barbara Turner Vesselago, my freefall instructor. Thank you Barbara for starting me on my writing journey.

Barbara Olsen, my daughter, the artist. Thank you for your beautiful book cover illustration, for the illustrations within the book, and for your patience and support.

Dawn Keer, my editor. Thank you for your excellent editing, encouragement and enthusiasm.

Gwen Molnar, my friend, and a published author. Many thanks for reading my manuscript and for your suggestions and encouragement.

Sheila Masson, a long-time friend who has always encouraged me to have my writing published. Thank you for reading my manuscript.

Ed Olsen, my supportive husband, and a fun traveling companion. I'm so happy that you also love to go to Bruges.

Works Cited

Bouchardon, Patrice. *The Healing Energy of Trees.* Boston, MA: Journey Editions, 1999. Print.

Campbell, Joseph, and Bill Moyers. "Myth and the Modern World." *The Power of Myth.* Ed. Betty Sue Flowers. New York: Anchor Books, 1991. 5. Print.

Mayes, Frances. *Under the Tuscan Sun: at Home in Italy.* New York: Broadway Books, 1997. Print.

M argaret Olsen taught elementary school for a number of years and also a journaling course for adults. She has raised four children and enjoys travelling, especially to Bruges, Belgium. Margaret has been writing fiction and creative non-fiction since 1990. She and her husband live in Edmonton, Alberta.